Transgressing Teacher Education

Transgressing Teacher Education

Strategies for Equity, Opportunity, and Social Justice in Urban Teacher Preparation and Practice

Alice E. Ginsberg

ROWMAN & LITTLEFIELD
Lanham • Boulder • New York • London

Published by Rowman & Littlefield
An imprint of The Rowman & Littlefield Publishing Group, Inc.
4501 Forbes Boulevard, Suite 200, Lanham, Maryland 20706
www.rowman.com

86-90 Paul Street, London EC2A 4NE, United Kingdom

British Library Cataloguing in Publication Information Available

Library of Congress Cataloging-in-Publication Data

Name: Ginsberg, Alice E., author.
Title: Transgressing teacher education : strategies for equity, opportunity and social justice in urban teacher preparation and practice / Alice E. Ginsberg.
Description: Lanham, Maryland : Rowman & Littlefield, 2022. | Includes bibliographical references and index. | Summary: "This book is a series of original strategies that teacher educators, teacher candidates and practicing teachers can use to think critically about issues of equity, diversity, opportunity, and social justice in urban education"—Provided by publisher.
Identifiers: LCCN 2021046338 (print) | LCCN 2021046339 (ebook) | ISBN 9781475865233 (cloth) | ISBN 9781475865240 (paperback) | ISBN 9781475865257 (epub)
Subjects: LCSH: Teachers—Training of—United States. | Education, Urban—United States. | Educational equalization—United States. | Social justice and education—United States.
Classification: LCC LB1715 .G468 2022 (print) | LCC LB1715 (ebook) | DDC 370.71/1—dc23/eng/20211022
LC record available at https://lccn.loc.gov/2021046338
LC ebook record available at https://lccn.loc.gov/2021046339

♾ ™ The paper used in this publication meets the minimum requirements of American National Standard for Information Sciences Permanence of Paper for Printed Library Materials, ANSI/NISO Z39.48-1992.

This book is dedicated to Lisa Bennett and Cathy Yun, two truly inspirational teacher educators, social justice warriors, and dear friends who have been a great inspiration to me. I didn't know how much I needed you both in my life until I met you.

Contents

Foreword

Andrea Honigsfeld

What does it mean to teach in the 21st century? What does teacher education look like in the age of continued systemic racism and discrimination? In her seminal work *Teaching to Transgress*, bell hooks (1994) cautioned of the dangers of educators using "the classroom to enact rituals of control that were about domination and the unjust exercise of power" (p. 5). Teacher educators are in no way immune to such oppressive practices, either; thus many researchers, policy makers, and practitioners agree that radical changes to preservice teacher preparation are long overdue. Alice Ginsberg powerfully builds on hooks's legacy and fiercely argues for transgressing false narratives about race, politics, and education, and challenges her readers to overcome systemic inequities perpetuated by teacher education. She powerfully calls for immediate action to ensure that urban teacher preparation fully embraces equity, opportunity, and social justice education.

In the forthcoming pages, Alice Ginsberg gives voice to many of my own long-held professional intuitions and beliefs about preservice teacher preparation. I wholeheartedly cheer her on as she invites her readers to:

- Fully focus on their own and their students' complex identities
- Define their positionality as educators
- Ensure representation across groups in all instructional settings
- Embrace strength- rather than deficit-based instructional practices in their classrooms
- Address issues of systemic racism and educational inequity head on

This type of advocacy for change is akin to what Bettina Love (2019) calls abolitionist teaching, the cornerstone of which is intentional refocusing on mattering. Love defined *mattering* as a quest for humanity and a way to recognize the importance and dignity of everyone's intersectional identities. She claimed that fully understanding and enacting mattering to ourselves, to each other, to our communities, and to the larger society creates a pathway to achieving freedom from oppression. Reproducing existing oppressive, discriminatory, and unjust practices in our classrooms and schools hurt some of the most vulnerable children and their families. The alternative is to reimagine schools and redefine the future of teacher education!

Alice Ginsberg also recognizes that it is not an easy job to dismantle existing structures of privilege and oppression in teacher education and beyond: it requires solid conceptual understanding and accessible, actionable strategies, both of which she skillfully presents throughout the nine chapters of this book. What I most appreciate about the vision, the research-informed framework, and the practical application of Ginsberg's transformational work is how she unapologetically accomplishes all of the following while consistently making the case that there are no other viable alternatives for society to move forward:

- Relentless interrogation of underlying core values, current beliefs, and perceived best practices
- Systematic integration of seminal and current critical research
- Rejection of a pedagogical focus on students through a deficiency lens
- Full embrace of and honoring each member's humanity in our educational communities

I am convinced that readers will find themselves slowing down to fully take in Ginsberg's carefully supported claims, clearly presented arguments, and poignantly illustrated strategies. They will read vigorously and pause frequently, as I did, to be affirmed at times and challenged at others, let their reflections turn into new convictions, and find urgently needed teacher preparation practices that will challenge the status quo.

REFERENCES

hooks, b. (1994). *Teaching to transgress: Education as the practice of freedom.* Routledge.
Love, B. (2019). *We want to do more than survive: Abolitionist teaching and the pursuit of educational freedom.* Beacon Press.

Preface

Balancing on the Invisible Wires of Promise

"Every day I feel that I am suspended in the air, being held up by thin invisible wires of promise, hope, and the belief that what I am doing is the right thing for my students. My fear is that one day I will realize that these wires are none of those things. My fear is that I am being held up by the very things I am hoping to be working against—the status quo, the oppression of my students and their communities—and the belief that there is no hope in education today is true."—Ashley, urban teacher education candidate

The above quote from one of my teacher candidate's journals has haunted me for a long time. It exemplifies the fear that many social justice–oriented teacher candidates and practicing teachers think that, without active support and interventions, they will be swallowed up by the status quo and become part of the very problem they set out to solve. While teacher education programs have begun to recognize the need to directly address issues of systemic racism and educational inequity, it is still the case that many candidates are frustrated because the central "narratives" comprising their preparation are misaligned with their daily experiences in the classroom. Such is the case of one former teacher candidate of mine, Sarah, who wrote in her journal:

The fact that some students survive such a brutal system is a testament to miracle, and their own tenacity, strength, and beyond-the-odds kind of experience. So very little of what I've daily experienced of the school system seems to set them up for survival, much less success. As teachers, the narratives being fed to us about who we are, who we should be, who are students are, and who they should be do not seem to align with many people's daily experiences.

Over the last decade, a wealth of research and publications in the field of teacher education has begun to seek out and highlight counternarratives that reflect the real challenges and dilemmas that face teachers, especially teachers of color and those who work in low-income, urban schools comprised primarily of students of color. These counternarratives are often accompanied by concrete suggestions for resistance, transformation, and systemic change. This book seeks to complement these resources with a series of original strategies, reflective assignments, critical questions, and transgressive voices that teacher educators can use or adapt to help candidates disrupt the status quo of teacher preparation and practice through:

- Critically reflecting on the candidate's own identities, positionality, and privilege.
- Deconstructing and analyzing the working politics, discourses, and ideologies inherent in the classrooms and school communities in which they are learning to teach.
- Challenging traditional deficit-based assumptions about equity, inclusion and culture that can impede and silence students from minoritized communities.
- Transgressing false narratives of Whiteness, meritocracy, and assimilation that too often anchor or define teacher education coursework and pedagogy.

I created and used these strategies in my own work as a teacher educator in an urban teacher education master's program located at a university on the East Coast. The candidates in my class were teaching during the day in urban schools while doing their formal teacher preparation coursework during evenings and on weekends. My course was a two-semester capstone called "Inquiry into Practice," which culminated in candidates' original practitioner inquiry projects. Candidates in my class constructed their own research questions and used their own schools, classrooms, colleagues, and students to investigate them. Through this process, they also sought to challenge static ways of thinking about teaching and learning, while publicly calling out practices that perpetuated inequity and disengagement in their own workplace.

When I was first asked to teach this class, however, a quick look at the syllabi of previous iterations immediately raised some troubling questions for me. There was a lot of emphasis on the methodological "tools" of practitioner inquiry, but very little attention paid to the *politics* of engaging in this kind of work. Teachers who position their own students and colleagues at the center of their critical inquiry risk upsetting overt and covert hierarchies in their schools. Many times, this means being the first one to challenge an injustice, disrupt the taken-for-granted, or even just break a long-held silence. While the candidates in my class hoped to make some of these assumptions and biases more transparent through their inquiry, they clearly feared personal repercussions for doing so in the schools they worked in. As one of my candidates reflected:

> Regardless of the rules and policies that govern the way my school operates, I have a firm belief that I will be fair with my students and that fairness will triumph over any policy in place. However, each week I am faced with struggles that stem from my reluctance to conform to policies—seemingly those set in stone—that are just downright unfair to students. I grapple with students in order to make them conform to policies I do not believe in, and I grapple with administration because I feel forced to facilitate policies that I do not believe in.

I feel forced to facilitate policies that I do not believe in. Let's pause and reflect on that statement for a minute. Imagine deciding to go into teaching, a profession known to have low salaries and not much respect. Then imagine committing to teaching in an underfunded urban school district with exceptionally large teacher-student ratios, lack of materials and resources, dilapidated and unsafe buildings, and a high number of "underachieving" and "underserved" students. Then imagine completing years of education at great economic cost to become a certified teacher, including balancing coursework and student teaching with minimum-wage, often highly demanding jobs in the service sector. Imagine having to pay for and pass a series of high-stakes exams that only measure a small part of what makes a "good" teacher and that, upon failure, can literally test you out of teaching.

Imagine getting hired in an urban school district despite multiple rounds of layoffs, strikes, and changes in your local school district and school administration. Imagine facing multiple reform mandates such as No Child Left Behind (NCLB), Race to the Top (RTTT), and Common Core without access to the necessary professional development or resources to fulfil these mandates. Most of all, imagine thinking you are going through all this because you want to be *that teacher*, the person who is instrumental to ensuring educational equity, challenging systemic racism, and creating opportunities for your students to engage and excel. Then imagine standing in front of those students and thinking to yourself *I feel forced to facilitate policies that I do not believe in.*

This belief was not uncommon among the scores of teacher candidates I worked with over the years. Many of the candidates I worked with seemed very conflicted about their role in the classroom and in students' lives, especially when it came to issues of control, as evidenced in the uncomfortable question mark at the end of this candidate's journal entry:

> I write frequently about how little control my students have over their day. They have very little choice in their classes, almost no social time, strict rules and regulations that dictate what they can wear, when they can eat, how they sit in class. If they have such little power, it almost seems natural that they would try to fight us for some of that back. *I suppose that is at least better than learned helplessness?*

The constant pressure to have classrooms that always appeared to be orderly and "on task" led many candidates I worked with to lament the resulting loss of building individualized and meaningful relationships with their students, such as the candidate who reflected, "In cramming to prepare the best lessons I possibly could, driven to close the achievement gap for my kids, I lost sight of building the relationships and trust necessary to be a transformational teacher."

Indeed, the candidates in my courses expressed their frustrations in every way possible, as evidenced by the recurring questions in their journals: *Why do I expect my students to be interested in what I'm teaching if I'm not interested? How do I address students' feelings of negativity and defeat? What do I do when I see students treated unfairly? How do I get students to question what is going on around them? How can I speak up without endangering my job or my "reputation" with other teachers? How do I find my place in a school where I feel very out of place? How can I support my students when I myself do not feel supported? What is the difference between simply "dealing" with a problem and finding a solution? Can we change the systems that we teach in? Should we try or put our energies elsewhere?*

Every year I got a new group of teacher candidates, and every year some version of these same questions came to light. While all of these questions disturbed me, the last question—*of whether to stay in teaching or put their energies elsewhere*—was always the pervasive elephant in the room. I could not ignore that, over the years, I saw many of the candidates in my classes leave teaching altogether, while others soldiered on, in their own words "feeling more disingenuous with each passing day." This seemed to be particularly true for candidates of color. For example, one candidate in my class wrote in her journal about taking student failure "more personally" than many of her co-workers:

> I believe as a person of color I am extremely frustrated because I see the reality for the community I serve, and I know that the students can rise above their circumstances with proper support. I feel like I take student failure more personally than most of my co-workers, and it is hard to challenge the accepted inferiority accepted by the adults and students. The system is set up to keep poor people of color disempowered and just content with surviving.

This same candidate later wrote about her own feelings of being held to a different standard than her White counterparts:

> Based on the experiences of fellow black teachers, I feel like the accepted stereotype of us as being hostile, overly opinionated, or difficult to please decides how the administration allows us to use our voice. As black teachers we are expected to be better capable of grinning and bearing the challenges and it is less acceptable for me to struggle.

Many other teachers of color have expressed similar feelings, leading to an expansion of research about the low retention rates and "invisible tax" associated with teachers of color. Research suggests that one of the primary reasons that teachers of color leave the profession is that they feel silenced and unable to successfully advocate for student equity (Achinstein, et al., 2010; Carver-Thomas, 2018; Kohli 2018, 2021). As Jackson and Kohli (2016, p. 6) bluntly state: "We are recruiting teachers of Color into spaces where they are limited, dehumanized, and alienated from their professional identity and goals." In my experience, many teacher candidates also felt "silenced" in their schools and classrooms. I kept thinking about another one of my candidates who felt forced into silence and believed that advocating for her students meant that her very survival as a teacher was threatened. She wrote:

> The most prevalent issues in my journal revolve around the choices my administration makes that go against what I feel is best for students. These choices are often made without teacher input, and I feel bullied to be silent and compliant. Normally, I am a very vocal person, but I realized just how silencing my job has become based on the way I express how disempowered I feel. The environment I work in has forced me to be silent as a means of survival.

Pause here and reflect again: *The environment I work in has forced me to be silent as a means of survival.*

As Dana and Yendol-Hoppey (2020, p. 39) suggest, survival and success in the teaching profession are often at odds with each other and that "keeping teachers in teaching is not the same as helping them become good teachers." This contradiction rang especially true to me. The reality that the candidates in my course were being forced to facilitate policies and practices they did not believe in and were being forced to be silent as a means of survival became somewhat of a Catch-22 for me as a teacher educator. I wanted to encourage my candidates to become change agents who were not afraid to wrestle with the conflicts and dilemmas that would inevitably arise for them. However, I also wanted to arm them with the knowledge and tools they would need to "survive" against what I knew would be heavy opposition in many of the schools where they taught or would teach.

I especially grappled with questions and statements from my candidates about whether they should stay in teaching or try to "make a difference" some other way. One candidate asked: "Is immediate academic success worth me sacrificing my own personal values as a teacher and my students' freedom of behavior and choice?" Good question. So, was my goal to help the students in my class become "good teachers," defined herein as those who challenge inequities, uproot systemic racism, and put their future students' interests first? Or was it simply to acclimate them to the realities of teaching in a broken system and help them survive in this system? Or was there something in-between? As a teacher educator, reflecting on these questions did not feel optional. I had to live with myself at the end of every class and every day.

Critical questions I asked my candidates to reflect on in their weekly journals were: "What questions remain most salient in my thoughts? What questions, if any, have I decided *not* to address and why? What questions do I need the most help with? How can I find that help?" What could I say to the candidate who responded:

> The questions that remain most salient in my thoughts are the questions based around teachers and why they choose to do the work that they do. I hear way too often that in order for education to improve more people who feel strongly about education ought to be in front of the classroom. I believe this to be true to an extent, but it seems like teachers are not valued in schools anymore. Schools seem to want people who do not care about the students they serve because, as a passionate teacher who really wants to do well, I constantly feel struck down or not supported. Learning more about the most affirming parts of teaching will motivate me to either continue with my teaching career or stop before I am too deep in to ever get out.

Or what about the candidate who wrote:

> My journal has brought up many questions for me. For example, how can I affirm my students' identity and self-esteem? How do I address systemic issues to students and develop a space for them to develop opinions? How can I facilitate the development of my students' consciousness? How do I get them to question what is going on around them? I want my students to be critical about the information they receive, but I do not know how I can spare time for thought provoking discussions with the school's push toward increasing test scores. Furthermore, I don't know if I can address the issues with administration without any repercussions.

My ultimate answer to these kinds of questions is reflected in the title of this book. It is time to *Transgress Teacher Education*. I believe that in order for education to be truly transformational for our future students, teacher education has to be equally transformational for our future teachers. At the heart of this book is the idea that we need to keep developing counter-narratives not just in teaching and in education, but in *teacher education*. In the spirit of bell hooks' transformative body of work on teaching and learning as a "practice of freedom" and her call for *Teaching to Transgress*, this book provides innovative yet practical and accessible strategies for teacher educators who want to change the narratives that comprise teacher education and empower their candidates to "practice freedom" in their preparation and clinical practice.

Of course, the idea of "changing" or "reforming" traditional approaches to teacher education is nothing new. As far back as 1992, Mary Dilworth edited the book *Diversity in Teacher Education: New Expectations* in which contributors Nelson-Barber and Mitchell (1992, p. 254) boldly stated that: "If we want to influence student teachers to teach in new ways, we must use those ways in teaching them." Subsequent research and publications by practitioners and pioneers in teacher education reform have presented us with many new models and mandates, such as the importance of integrating culturally responsive pedagogy and critical race theory across the teacher education curriculum; bridging gaps between content and methods coursework; increasing and foregrounding candidate practice in authentic and diverse school settings; utilizing mentoring and cohort models; building mutually beneficial and non-hierarchical university-school-community partnerships; adopting inquiry as stance and practice-based teacher education. *Transgressing teacher education* is grounded in all of these ideas, and I am indebted to the work of my colleagues who have shaped me as a teacher educator and inspired me to create many of the strategies in this book for my own students. I am also indebted to the candidates in my courses, as their candid feedback helped me to refine these strategies and to look for gaps where new strategies were needed.

Bottom line: In order to transgress teacher education, teacher educators must be intentional about modeling new ways of teaching teacher candidates. It is my hope that the strategies can contribute to this mission. For this reason, I have designed this book to be more of a "workbook" than a theory or textbook. It is my hope that those who use it will write in it and not be discouraged when things get "messy" as they will almost certainly become. These strategies can be used in any teacher education program (traditional or alternative) and can be used in sequence or independently. While questions at the end of chapter offer ways that teacher educators and candidates can engage in group discussions, the strategies in this book can also be adapted by individual candidates and in-service teachers who want to further reflect on their own practice. This book reflects my firm belief that teaching and learning are synonymous activities, and that as teacher educators we must model this for our students, who then must model it for their future students.

Finally, in response to Ashley's journal entry quoted at the beginning of this preface, I avow that there is in fact hope in education today, but that hope needs to be grounded in the reality of an inequitable and discriminatory system that has promoted the status quo long enough. It is time to try something different and without being forced to facilitate policies we don't believe in and without being silenced as a means of survival. We must keep balancing on those "thin, invisible wires of promise" until we are being held up by the very things we are working for: equity, opportunity, and social justice.

Acknowledgments

I would like to thank my colleagues at the University of Pennsylvania and Rutgers University for providing me with the opportunity and freedom to teach in ways that felt authentic and transgressive, and which led me to develop many of the strategies in this book.

I'd also like to thank my students, who never cease to surprise me with their care, candor, courage, and commitment, not to mention their perseverance. I received meaningful feedback on the strategies in this book. Many of them also agreed to be quoted in this book, and their voices are a critical part of the narrative.

I'd like to thank Marybeth Gasman for including me in such original and transformative research, programming, presentations, and publications over many years. Working with you has been one of the great pleasures of my life. Being your good friend is also high on that list.

I would like to thank Andrew Martinez, who read the manuscript several times and is a wonderful editor, activist, and scholar who is certainly going to make a positive difference in the world.

I would like to thank my colleague Andrea Honigsfeld for writing the foreword and Julia Katz Terry for her beautiful cover art.

Of course, I want to thank my husband, Jason Zisser, who not only listens to me talk about my work and contributes to my ideas but never fails to make me smile. You have brought so much joy and happiness into my life.

Lastly, to Nick, Andrew, Lee, Declan, and Zoe. Our family has grown considerably in the last decade, and although we are a crazy bunch, I love you all so very much.

Introduction

Transgressing Teacher Education

"If institutional racism permeates schools including the curriculum, how can teacher educators recruit, prepare, and support those who will resist it?"— Sleeter, 2016, p. 1066

As the U.S. student population grows increasingly racially, culturally, and linguistically diverse, and as the achievement and opportunity gaps for poor students and students of color continue to widen, our teacher education programs are not keeping pace. Most prominently, both teacher educators *and* teacher candidates are over 80% White, and 40% of students will never have a teacher of color. While teacher education programs must continue to aggressively recruit teacher educators and candidates of color, however, the issue is not simply one of finding a demographic balance, or what has been called "the demographic imperative" (Banks, 1995).

Of course, we need to diversify the teaching profession. The research on the positive impact of having teachers of color in the classroom is compelling and growing all the time. This research underscores that teachers of color serve as positive role models for students of color and provide needed examples of people in color in positions of intellectual prowess and authority for White students. Research also suggests that teachers of color generally hold higher expectations for students of color, are more likely to reach out to students' families and communities for consultation and support, recognize the rich array of cultural assets and "funds of knowledge" that students of color bring to the classroom, are committed to changing unfair discipline and tracking policies, and use a wider array of assessments (beyond standardized tests) to measure student learning (Villegas & Irvine, 2010; Ladson-Billings,

2011; Nieto, 2000; Noguera, 2008; Milner and Howard, 2013; Picower 2009; Zeichner 2009; Gasman et al. 2016).

Regardless of how many candidates of color we attract into the teaching profession, however, the design and curriculum of most teacher education programs are still centered in Whiteness (Tolbert & Eichelberger, 2014; Burciaga & Kohli, 2018; Hambacher & Ginn 2021) and reflect what Sleeter (2017) has called "white sensibilities." What this means is that attention to "multicultural issues" is usually reified in the form of one or two separate courses which, according to Sleeter (2017, p. 159), sends the message that knowledge of diversity is something that can be "bracketed off" from an otherwise White-centered curriculum. Yes, most teacher education programs have inserted the terms *equity*, *diversity* or *social justice* somewhere in their program and course descriptions, but what this actually means in practice is erratic and often surface-level (Ziechner, 2006; Sleeter, 2017; Milner, 2010; Hollins & Guzman, 2005). In most teacher education programs a "heroes and holidays" approach to culture still prevails, which can easily lead to reifying cultural stereotypes rather than refuting or reframing them (Grant and Gibson, 2011).

Moreover, many "diversity" courses fail to address and challenge the *systemic* causes of educational inequity by engaging candidates in critical and intersectional investigations of power and interest convergence. As Jackson and Kohli (2016, p. 4) found in their review of research on the experiences of teacher candidates of color: "Close examination of many teacher education programs reveal that respect for diversity is typically superficial and not supported by practices, instruction, curriculum, policies, and teacher dispositions." Commonly offered gateway and foundational teacher education courses with titles like "multicultural education" or "diverse issues in education" or "school and society" still focus disproportionately helping White candidates to identify and address their own privilege. While this is important work, it can be very alienating for candidates of color who are already acutely aware of systemic inequity, racial prejudice, and the trauma of racism, having experienced it across all the social institutions in their life (Pizarro & Kohli 2020). As Sleeter and Milner (2011, p. 88) remind us: "Implicitly most programs are designed mainly with traditional-age white students in mind, a reality that may be invisible to those in such programs but is visible to those who sense not belonging."

Tobert and Eichelberger (2014, p. 1) have further suggested that many candidates of color experience both microaggressions and "explicit and implicit messages about deference to the status quo" in their teacher education coursework and field placements. The authors further suggest that "institutional hierarchies" and "norms of professionalism" within teacher education programs can serve to silence dissenting voices, leading many teachers of color to report that their experiences were rarely elicited or valued. The authors posit that in addition to focusing on candidates becoming social justice teachers, teacher education programs need to focus inward, on becoming social justice *institutions*. This process, however, has proven to be quite controversial and has been met with significant resistance from other faculty members, administrators, and even some candidates.

Indeed, part of the persistence of diversity as an "add-on" approach is that traditional higher education faculty members have been schooled to believe that directly addressing issues of racism and systemic inequities in education brings politics where it does not belong. As bell hooks lamented nearly thirty years ago, professors are expected to be objective and free from any personal bias, and the self is "presumably emptied out" at the very instance professors enter the classroom (hooks, 1994, p. 17). Despite many current debates about the role of politics and activism in higher education the fear of "indoctrinating students" remains pervasive and has led to the suppression of discussion and content that might be highly charged or provocative, particularly those around race and racism (Katz & Rose, 2014; Apple 1996, 2012; Cammarota 2011; Hambacher & Ginn 2021).

As a result, many of the "narratives" and assumptions about quality teaching, intelligent students, and good schools that aspiring teachers are exposed to strive to be impartial and colorblind. Research on discussion of racism in teacher education, for example, led to Galman et al. (2010, p. 231) to conclude that in their experience fear of making White students uncomfortable led to "silencing race talk" and that "when conversations about race did occur, they seemed transitory, pro forma, or even panicked attempts to 'get it over with.'" Consequently, instead of addressing cultural bias and stereotyping, low-expectations, or pedagogies that are disengaging and detrimental to students, many teacher education programs focus instead on issues of individual intelligence, hard work, and grit, thus falsely portraying American schools and educational achievement as fair and meritocratic. These false narratives can be extremely disconcerting for teacher educators and candidates who do, in fact, see color, or more specifically, perceive systemic racism and widespread educational inequity in the schools and communities they live and will teach in.

It is also important to note that even those teacher educators that may be open to centering issues of racial injustice and interrupting false narratives around equity may be unsure of their qualifications and ability to do so. For one thing, as previously noted, the majority of teacher educators are themselves still primarily middle class and White, and many of them haven't recently *or ever* spent quality time in culturally and linguistically diverse school settings (Ladson-Billings, 2006). According to Hollins (2011, p. 106): "the majority of teacher educators have been socialized in much the same way as the candidates in their teacher education programs." As Galman et al. (2010, p. 227) further underscore, before we can ask preservice teachers to engage in meaningful conversations about race and equity "teacher educators must themselves experience what it means to grapple and connect that experience with their teacher education practice." bell hooks (1994, p. 142) likewise recalls of her own experience in the academy:

> Even those of us who are experimenting with progressive practices are afraid to change. Aware of myself as a subject in history, a member of a marginalized and oppressed group, victimized by institutionalized racism, sexism and class elitism, I had tremendous fear that I would teach in a manner that would reinforce those hierarchies. Yet I had absolutely no model, no example of what it would mean to enter a classroom and teach in a different way.

In institutions of higher education, faculty are also expected to be the experts on the subjects they teach and any hint of ceding this expertise can range from feeling simply new and uncomfortable to downright frightening and/or career-ending. According to hooks (p. 30), "Many folks found that as they tried to respect 'cultural diversity' they had to confront the limitations of their training and knowledge, as well as a possible loss of 'authority.'. . . A lot of people panicked." For faculty in higher education to critically question their own knowledge and pedagogy is more than simply emotionally and intellectually challenging; it can be accompanied by the very real risk that they may not have their contract renewed or are turned down for tenure and other promotions.

Moreover, it is not just other faculty and school administrators that can stand in judgement. hooks (p. 143) again warns: "The urge to experiment with pedagogical practices may not be welcomed by students who often expect us to teach in the manner they are accustomed to." In other words, when faculty enter the classroom as both active learners and participants, it can be seen as a sign of unpreparedness, intellectual inferiority, timidity, or even, ironically, not caring. Many students enter higher education expecting faculty to show care through a highly structured, inflexible, and paternalistic model of teaching.

All this does not mean that teacher education faculty members aren't serious about or committed to issues of educational equity. Many are actively trying to address social justice issues in their classrooms and in their candidates' clinical experiences. What this often means in practice, however, is that teacher educators: a) include token readings and curriculum materials on racism, equity, diversity and inclusion but do not ground these readings in on-going critical inquiry; b) ask candidates to reflect on their own cultural identity, privilege, and internal biases without tying them to systemic and intersectional inequities; and/or c) include a decontextualized school observation, service-learning or community engaged components to their course that unintentionally ends up confirming rather than refuting cultural stereotypes.

In other words, changing discrete aspects of the way one develops a syllabus or even teaches a course does not guarantee a more foundational shift in the way students learn and think. It is possible for a teacher candidate to reflect on their own unearned privilege, or to spend time "helping" in underserved communities, without ever disrupting underlying deficit narratives that can define and marginalize whole cultures. This is especially the case when majority students go into communities of color and take a savior or missionary approach or believe that they now know what it is like to be a minority. Being in the minority is not the same as being minoritized or being powerless. Furthermore, without explicit and guided reflection, candidates risk ignoring the funds of knowledge and cultural capital already in these communities.

Sleeter (2017, p. 158) reminds us that "It is difficult to shift the center of gravity of a program in which the center is defined by White interests, and any proposed change must align with White interests to gain support." Thus, Sleeter rightly concludes that addressing racism in teacher education must involve systemic and cultural changes in the institution of teacher education itself. Raising consciousness is an important start, but it has to lead to strategic and transgressive action. Power structures need to change. Silences need to be broken. According to Galman et al. (2010, p. 234) systemic change requires us to create spaces in teacher education "where whiteness can be named and interrogated" and where "all students and faculty can craft new, transformative understandings of themselves and their work." Until we fulfil this promise, teacher education will continue to be centered in Whiteness. As hooks (1994, p. 147) rightly notes: "Education as the practice of freedom is not just about liberatory knowledge, it's about a liberatory practice in the classroom."

In the tradition of hooks' *Teaching to Transgress* the chapters in this book bridge critical reflection with strategic and *transgressive* action. The chapters that follow all begin with a discussion of the theoretical concepts and goals of the strategy and are followed by critical refection questions. The strategies in the chapters to follow can be adapted and used in traditional or alternative teacher education programs, as well as for the professional development and continuous growth of practicing teachers. They do not have to be done in sequence, although they do build upon each other. Perhaps most importantly, each chapter ends with transgressive voices of real teacher candidates as they grapple with race, equity and social justice in theory and in practice. *Following is a brief outline of each of the chapters and activities within them.*

Chapter 1 focuses on issues of identity and intersectionality. It is important that aspiring and practicing teachers reflect critically on how they construct and project their own identity standpoints, while they begin to look at their students in more multidimensional and intersectional ways. The concept of intersectionality is fundamental and foundational to understanding diversity, discrimination, and structural racism. Intersectionality underscores the ways in which race, class and gender (as well as many other identities such as sexual orientation, religion, and nationality) cannot be fully understood in isolation and that even those who are oppressed in some areas can be privileged in others. Yet, while the term itself stresses the movement, joining and overlay of "intersections," it has nonetheless been criticized as creating yet more static and essentialist identity categories. For this reason, the activity in chapter 1 asks teacher candidates to think critically not only about how they *identify* themselves, but also how they *position* themselves in relation to these identities, and how they *represent* these identities in different contexts. Candidates will fill out a multi-layered identity mapping chart. Through this process, candidates are asked to reflect on how their identities, positions and representations are not stagnant; they can and do shift over time and across contexts.

Chapter 2 seeks to challenge and transgress deficit models and orientations of students by focusing on what Tara Yosso (2005) has called community cultural wealth. Candidates create a personal "collage" of their own community cultural wealth using Yosso's six categories of capital: *aspirational, navigational, social, familiar, linguistic*, and *resistant*. The term "collage" is defined very loosely, as candidates are encouraged to use any markers they choose, ranging from: family photos, videos, illustrations, advertisements, poems, tapestries, recipes, diaries, and folk tales, to actual spoken word performances, dances, simulations, or demonstrations. Critical questions guide candidates through the process of using similar collages to recognize their own students' diverse funds of knowledge, and to use their community cultural wealth to create an asset-based pedagogy across the curriculum.

Chapter 3 explores common terms used in educational discourse about student achievement, such as "at-risk," "underserved," "model minority," and "special education." These Discourses come laden with explicit and implicit assumptions and preconceptions that often go unmarked or unquestioned. (Discourse is purposely capitalized here to underscore the politicized nature of language.) The term "achievement gap," for example, has been especially persistent in educational Discourse to describe underachieving students, although some educators have suggested the true problem is more of an "opportunity gap," and/or an "action gap." Critical Discourse Analysis (CDA) highlights the ways in which language and choice of words reflect larger ideologies about power and privilege. In this activity, candidates are asked to select quotes about education drawn from diverse sources: magazines and newspapers, educational politicians and funders, school administrators, school reform researchers, among others. CDA is then applied to each quote, to carefully consider how the wording choices and emphasis reflect overt and hidden assumptions about teaching and learning. It is not enough to simply call attention to these Discourses. Critical questions at the end of the chapter prompt candidates to think about why certain ideologies and Discourses are more believable or effective than others.

Chapter 4 prompts teacher candidates to consider the ways in which intelligence is frequently a culturally constructed category that is defined by students' public display of cultural norms and expectations in the classroom. As Hatt (2012) found in her ethnographic study of kindergarten students, definitions of individual smartness were found to be inherent in classroom-based pedagogies of control and social positioning and further argues that smartness is "not just an ideology or belief but an actual practice: more verb than noun." Hatt further identifies how particular artifacts in the classroom—such as a traffic light that constantly displays which students are acting out—creates a "figured world" where smartness became a "collective event" in which students are positioned against each other in order to justify and reify power hierarchies based on race and class. The activity in this chapter helps candidates reflect, record, codify, and rethink their interactions with students and internal biases, surrounding the issue of smartness and intelligence.

Chapter 5 was inspired by a progressive, inquiry and project-based learning high school in Philadelphia called the Science Leadership Academy (SLA). SLA's mission statement is, in fact, a series of questions: *How do we learn? What can we create? What does it mean to lead?* A school mission statement that begins with questions invites a multiplicity of voices and perspectives, invites the co-creation of values, and challenges a static and hierarchical notion of purpose. This chapter prompts candidates to identify and codify existing school mission statements, *and then turn them into questions*. After being guided through this process, this chapter provides a series of prompts enabling candidates to critically reflect on how the mission of the school is transformed by using questions, and to think about the "consequences" and transgressive possibilities of allowing teachers, students, and other educational stakeholders to co-create school missions.

Chapter 6, building on the strategies in chapter 5, provides a bridge between looking at school mission statements to observing schools' actual living cultures. The activity and corresponding critical questions were inspired by Sam Chaltain's book *American Schools* (2009), in which he promotes the recognition that schools are not machines, but rather are "complex, living systems." Chaltain urges educators interested in school reform to uncover the hidden curriculum, and to make the invisible visible by asking: "If the shared culture of the school I visited was a *living thing*, what would it look, feel, and act like? If that living thing could talk, what would it say to us? If it could develop, what would it morph into next?" Chapter 6 provides candidates with a series of guided school observation experiences and questions, followed by an original reflection on what it means to view schools as "living entities" or dynamic communities, as opposed to simply a building, institution, or commodity.

Chapter 7 focuses on deconstructing school policies that are specifically designed to control and regulate student movement and expression. While ever popular policies like sitting *criss-cross applesauce*, or having students walking down the hallway *hip and lip* (e.g., with one hand on their hip and one hand on their lip) may seem non-controversial, this chapter raises critical questions about the control of student bodies and the practices of compliance and "restraint." While many of these policies seem *on the surface* to be about student/school safety, focus, or self-regulation, students do not necessarily internalize them in positive or motivational ways and in fact, often "act out" because of them. This chapter prompts candidates to identify and critically deconstruct rules about "movement" in schools—especially as it relates to issues of class, race, gender and sexuality—as well as to think about how diverse students perceive these movements, and what it would mean to "re-choreograph" them.

Chapter 8 guides candidates through the process of using metaphors and design thinking to consider competing stakeholder perspectives on change and the "interests" that underlie what is considered a productive or dysfunctional solution to educational problems. Design thinking is an iterative process which seeks to unearth standard patterns of problem solving, replacing them with novel solutions where the roots of knowledge are constantly being called into question and creators are asked to emphasize and see the world through the eyes of their users. In this case, educational policymakers need to think about how schools and teachers enact policies, and teachers need to think about how their students are experiencing these policies. Using student achievement as a foundational issue that policymakers address, this chapter prompts candidates to engage in design thinking as well as to consider who stands to gain (or loose) from diverse alternate solutions.

The conclusion serves as a call to action, detailing specific ways that we might transgress current models of teacher education without abandoning them altogether. It is important to state this specifically because there has been increasing momentum to get rid of traditional teacher education programs in higher education and replace them with alternative routes. Without judging the individual merits of these alternative routes, traditional teacher education programs at colleges and universities have a lot to offer candidates and preparing teachers is something that cannot and should not be rushed. That models for teacher education are always evolving is a good thing, but we must be wary of attempts to treat teacher preparation as purely a "training" program. Ongoing and integrated reflection, practice and reflection on practice must remain at the center of teacher preparation. This final chapter addresses some concrete ways we can achieve this.

Chapter One

Intersectional Identity Mapping

*Strategy: Identity, Positionality,
and Representation Strategy*

"If in their desire to meet social justice, the instinct of prospective teachers may be to place PK-12 students (and everyone else) into these neat identity boxes, how might teacher educators scaffold their understandings and provide TCs [teacher candidates] a language of complexity. . . . It is not enough to acknowledge that multiple identities exist; instead, to fully prepare new teachers, we must actively engage these complex intersections."—Pugach et al., 2019, p. 213

Key Concepts

Intersectionality, Identity, Positionality, and Representation

Goals

- Think critically about one's own cultural identity and standpoint, by reflecting on the categories of race, class, gender, sexuality, religion, nationality, language, education and other contributing factors that make up one's own construction of self and "other."
- Understand identity as a fluid, multidimensional, contextual, and intersectional process that is dependent upon context, positionality, and binaries of representation.
- Understand the ways in which how we identify ourselves internally is not always how others see or categorize us and vice versa.
- Consider ways in which aspects of our own identities can be optional, manipulated, cloaked, marginalized, or silenced.

- Become more critical of stereotyping students based on assumed or predicted identities.
- Learn to see and understand current and future students in more intersectional and multidimensional ways.

ABOUT INTERSECTIONALITY, IDENTITY, POSITIONALITY, AND REPRESENTATION

The ways in which we identify ourselves, and in which others see us, have a critical impact on both teaching and learning. Both teachers and students walk into the classroom with explicit and implicit assumptions about each other. We base these assumptions on skin color, binary representations of gender, students' first and last names, English language skills and accents, whether students are wearing a headscarf, hijab, Jewish star or cross necklace, whether they are wearing expensive sneakers or carrying a designer handbag, whether they are sitting in a wheelchair, whether they look too "old" for their assigned grade level, and many other factors.

While we used to see identity as something fixed or static, it is now generally accepted that "representation is a constant activity" which is embedded in specific social interactions and in specific contexts (Danielewicz, 2001, p. 168). A common word for this is intersectionality, which means that different parts of our identity literally "intersect" with each other, framing the way we are perceived by others and the way we perceive ourselves. While intersectionality may have become something of a "buzz word" in academic and political circles, it is nonetheless fundamental and foundational to anyone who seeks to understand diversity, discrimination, and structural racism.

The term intersectionality was coined by feminist law scholar Kimberlé Crenshaw in 1989, and later made more prominent by feminist scholar Patricia Hill Collins—both Black women—who sought to challenge the idea that the experiences of White middle-class women were representative of *all* women. Intersectionality underscores the fact that social markers like race, class and gender cannot be fully understood in isolation and, furthermore, that those who are oppressed in some areas can still be privileged in others. From a legal perspective, this is especially significant because it can serve to completely marginalize the interests of people who are at the crossroads.

Crenshaw, for example, explains how Black women are often excluded from racial discrimination lawsuits because the companies being sued hire Black men *and* excluded from gender discrimination lawsuits because the companies being sued hire White women. It is also important to note here that intersectionality is not just about race and gender, despite them being the most visible identities and being at the center of many discourses around discrimination. Identities such as sexual orientation, religion, ethnicity, and nationality have also been named as critical to understanding the ways in which we construct the categories of "self" and "other."

Even though the term *intersectionality* stresses the movement, joining and overlay of "intersections," it has nonetheless been criticized as creating yet more static identity categories as many people approach intersectionality as a kind of "identity stacking" or laundry list that does not reflect the multiple levels of scale at which each axis operates simultaneously (individual, inter-personal, institutional, and structural). For this reason, the activity in chapter 1 asks candidates to think not only about how they identify themselves but how they *position* themselves in relation to each identity, and how their individual and group identities are actively lived (or "represented") in specific contexts, epistemologies and ontologies.

The activity in this chapter stands out from similar activities, such as McIntosh's (1989) iconic "Invisible Knapsack" (in which she lists all of the explicit and implicit privileges she holds as a White woman in a racist society) or the "Privilege Walk" activity (wherein students take a step forwards or backwards depending on whether they possess a particular privilege), in that it seeks to help teacher candidates critically link *identity* and *privilege* with *positionality* and *representation*. In other words, we may consciously or unconsciously possess privileges that come with certain identities, but how we came to hold these identities and privileges, how we actively "claim" or refute them, and how we "utilize" them and represent them in different contexts is both deeply personal and deeply political. We use the terms such as "White people" and "people of color," for example, suggesting that White is not a color, or that White people are not raced. Likewise, many people feel that race and ethnicity is something they cannot "hide" or "opt out of" (even though skin color is not always a true representation of race and ethnicity), in contrast to social class which is an identity that they can manipulate, control, change, and/or subsume by dressing in a certain way or driving an expensive car.

Of course, in many cases what one feels or believes about their identity (such as if it is a "choice") may not matter in terms of how this identity is defined and accepted in the larger contexts of power and politics. Identities shift in relation to representations of dominance, center, or normality. As Pugach et al. (2019, p. 214) note: "Probing the complexity of multiple identities can . . . help candidates understand how risk is amplified based on multiple jeopardies." It is important that future and practicing teachers not only understand how they construct and project their own identity standpoints in the classroom, but also that they begin to look at their students in more multidimensional and intersectional ways.

The strategy in this chapter leads candidates through the process of generating a personal, multidimensional map of their intersecting *identities, positionalities,* and *representations.* A series of critical questions follows, designed to help candidates unpack and deconstruct the ways in which representation is a constant activity that is embedded in the flow of specific interactions. Among the critical questions that candidates are asked to reflect on is: "When, how and in what contexts do your identities shift? Are some identity categories more likely to shift than others?"

INSTRUCTIONS FOR FILLING OUT AN IDENTITY MAP

Step One

The outermost circle represents different ways that people categorize or classify themselves and others. Feel free to add other categories that you feel are significant. Also, you may decide to change the wording of the categories but be sure to notate why.

Step Two

In the next layer, you should make notes as to how *you personally* identify within each category. For example, under the category of race, you might write: *Black, African American, person of color*, or all three. Also note that your response may be singular, or multiple, as people are bi-racial, bi-lingual, or have more than one religion. *If you are uncomfortable or resistant for any reason, you can leave any category blank but be sure to think about why you made this decision.*

Step Three

In the next layer, you should consider *your positionality* within each category. Positionality refers to a wide range of ways that we relate to and think about our different identities, such as:

- chosen/inherited
- visible/invisible
- comfortable/uncomfortable
- sure/unsure
- stagnant/shifting
- distinct/overlapping
- authentic/misperception
- proud/ashamed

There are many other positions; these are just meant to get you started.

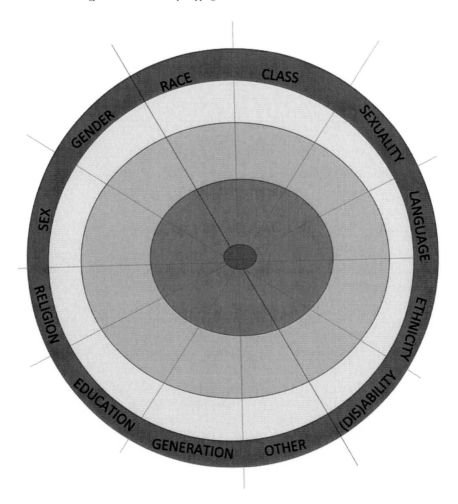

Intersectional Identity Mapping.

Step Four

In the next layer, you will be reflecting on "representation." How does this identity exist in the "self/other" continuum? You should write down what you believe to be the "dominant" identity in each category in the United States. You can define "dominant" as you want, and you can use different measures for different identities. For example:

- demographic majority

- access to power, privilege, and opportunity
- identities that are assumed to be the "norm" (e.g., astronaut vs. woman astronaut)
- recurring images in advertising and popular culture

Whatever you decide, be sure to notate how you chose and defined it as dominant for each category.

CRITICAL REFLECTION QUESTIONS

- Do your identities fit neatly into labeled categories like those prescribed in the outermost circles? Do some identities fit more easily than others? Why?
- Did you end up adding new identity categories, or renaming those that were preset? If so, why?
- How do different identities interrelate, intersect, exist in relation to, or stand at odds with each other? (For example, Jews may see Judaism as both an ethnicity and a religious identity. Some people may feel "queer" is both a gender identity and a sexual identity.) Did some identities "tug" at each other more than others?
- Thinking of positionality: how do you personally contribute to, or are forced into, these categories? Can you "opt out" of some identities but not others? Why/Why not?
- To what extent does your positionality match or clash with assumed outward perceptions of you? Can you think of an example of a time that someone misidentified you? What was happening?
- When, how and in what contexts do your identities shift? Are some identity categories more likely to shift than others?
- How did you determine what the dominant identity was? Did you use the same rationale/indicators of dominance for different categories? If not, what changed? Were there cases in which there were more than one dominant identity?
- What comforts and conflicts are associated with being or *not* being part of the dominant identity?

QUESTIONS FOR CLASSROOM DISCUSSION

- After sharing your identity charts, what surprised you the most about your classmates' maps?
- Were there identity categories you were more or less uncomfortable sharing?

- How does what you learned from this activity make you think differently about your future students?
- In light of this activity, what does it mean to attempt to build a culturally relevant curriculum or pedagogy?

TRANSGRESSIVE VOICES

In the following excerpts from their weekly course journals, three teacher candidates reflect on their intersectional identities and the impact of trying to "present" their authentic selves in the classroom. In the first excerpt Jannel talks about how difficult it was for her students to understand that she was an African American Muslim (born in Ethiopia) and not an Arab. In the second excerpt Peter talks about how, for most of his students, he was their first Asian American male teacher, prompting his students to think outside the Black/White dichotomy. In the third excerpt Maisha talks about being Nigerian American, born and raised in the suburbs of Maryland and how her students were quick to "misjudge" her. Taken together, these narratives illuminate the importance of engaging candidates in discussions about race in teacher education, while being cognizant of other key identities that intersect with and complicate racial assumptions and stereotypes.

Jannel

Ever since I started teaching last year, students always have questions about my life and where I come from. I don't fit into the African-American female archetype that students have built up in their minds. On the first day of school, I told my students that my family originated from Ethiopia, but I was born and raised in California. I also told them that I identify as African-American. Students talked about how I look Indian or just plain foreign. Some of their confusion stemmed from my headscarf; I didn't dress or look like all the other Philly Muslims who wore a headscarf, so I had to be Arab. We had this discussion in every class on that first day, yet every week since then students have been asking me "What are you? You're not Black!" It is baffling to me to hear students question what I have already told them as fact, and I have to continuously have this discussion with them for them to understand that not all African-Americans look the same, and that some people who identify as African-American are the 2nd or 3rd generation of their family here in this country.

My scarf has been a large point of discussion amongst the students. They all have theories about what my hair looks like. I haven't sat down and addressed this obsession of theirs because one reasoning behind wearing a headscarf is to be modest and not show off one's looks. Multiple times I have told my students that my hair is blue, I'm bald, or I use a sock to create my bun. Surprising, some students actually believe that I have blue hair. . . . How can I facilitate the development of my students' consciousness? How do I get them to question what is going on around them? I truly believe the beauty debate ties into issues of race and the historical construction of race. I want students to be critical about the information they receive, but I do not know how I can spare time for thought provoking discussions with the schools' push toward increasing testing scores.

Peter

Before I met my students last year, a vast majority of them had little understanding of race, ethnicity, and how to engage in conversation with a stranger about the two often aligned identity markers. If they did not have an Asian teacher—a teacher outside of the black-white dichotomy—an opportunity for those "conversations" probably would not have occurred.

The question of race is definitely the most salient feature of identity that came up in my class. Based on the demographics of our student body and the conversations I've had with a handful of students I think I can confidently say that I'm the only Asian person a strong majority of my students have had a prolonged relationship with. All throughout last year, a few students would yell "10 minute," "shrimp fried rice" and other Chinese food dishes in the middle of class.

That was the impetus for my discussion on the difference between race and ethnicity, as well as what prejudice was. This, in turn, created opportunities in talking about Trayvon Martin and Michael Brown and the preconceived ideas people have about young black people. After these conversations, I planned a lesson on what the terms "Latinx," "Spanish," and "Hispanic" meant and how the difference between race and ethnicity plays into these labels. I'm not too sure if this last lesson was the most successful one I've had, but I'm proud of the ways I found opportunities to speak about race and ethnicity as well as find opportunities for my students to learn more about me.

Maisha

I am a Nigerian-American, Marylander, female, Ivy-League educated, first born, born and raised in the suburbs, Christian, inner-city high school science educator. All of these identities are incredibility important to my life and to my work as a teacher. All of these identities have in some way impacted my teaching. As a first-year teacher, the most salient identities to me were my Nigerianness, the type of education I had, my socioeconomic background, and my hometown. These lines of difference were constantly shoved in my face whenever I interacted with my students the first year. I say shoved, because that's exactly what happened. My students would take these aspects of identities that I was proud of and would wield them as weapons. They were quick to judge or misjudge me according to those lines of differences, and these judgements had numerous implications. One of the most obvious implications is that I struggled greatly in the classroom during my first year of teaching. My reasons for my particular struggle were numerous. One struggle that I had during my first year of teaching was that I couldn't seem to figure out a way to live and teach in a way that was authentic to who I felt I was as an individual. I feel like I didn't have a space to be who I truly was.

Chapter Two

Asset-Based Teaching and Learning

*Strategy: Creating a Collage of
Cultural Capital and Community Wealth*

Teaching is an interpretive practice that requires knowledge of the community where students grow and develop, and where they are socialized"—Hollins and Guzman, 2005, p. 5

Key Concepts

Deficit Thinking, Funds of Knowledge, Culturally Relevant Pedagogy, and Community Cultural Wealth

Goals

- Challenge deficit perspectives of minoritized students and approach students from an asset-based perspective.
- Critically consider new frameworks and categories of students' cultural capital and community cultural wealth, especially those that represent the experiences and funds of knowledge of students of color.
- Expand definitions of student "knowledge" to include linguistic skills such as translating and code switching, resistance and counternarratives, sharing of cultural traditions and artifacts, and other "non-academic" forms of knowledge.
- Consider how knowledge and culture can be represented in multiple contexts and genres, including visual representation.

• Explore ways that expansive knowledge about students' funds of knowledge and community cultural wealth can inform culturally relevant teaching and learning.

ABOUT DEFICIT THINKING, FUNDS OF KNOWLEDGE, CULTURALLY RELEVANT PEDAGOGY, AND COMMUNITY CULTURAL WEALTH

When grappling with the "achievement gap," wherein students of color and low-income students perform poorly on standardized tests, are placed in lower academic tracks, are disproportionately punished for breaking school rules, and are more likely to drop out of school than their middle-class White peers, many policymakers and educators have fallen back on what is called "deficit thinking" (Davis and Museus, 2019; Valencia, 1997, 2010). Deficit thinking suggests that the problem lies in individual students' *motivation* (that they are lazy), *intelligence* (that they have lower IQs), *attitude* (that they are hostile or combative), or *resilience* (that they lack perseverance or "grit"). Deficit thinking can lead to teachers having low expectations for students when, in fact, many times the reasons why students appear to be "disengaged" is that they feel silenced, marginalized, and/or that the curriculum does not recognize or reflect their cultural knowledge and experiences. Deficit thinking also stems from White privilege and racial prejudice and stereotypes, wherein many teachers assume bad intent or disobedience from students of color, while viewing the same behaviors from White students as being engaged and proactive (Skiba & Williams, 2014; Noguera, 2008).

Importantly, deficit thinking often extends beyond individual students to negative assumptions about their families and/or cultural values. For example, students of immigrant parents who don't speak English are often accused of "not caring" about their child's education when in fact they are often unable to fully communicate with teachers due to language barriers. Parents of students from low-income families often are unable to attend school events and teacher conferences due to extended work schedules, and further lack the resources to fully support their children's educational success, such as home computers and internet access, tutoring and after school enrichment activities. African American parents, in particular, have been stereotyped as not caring about education, when in fact many of them have had such personal negative experiences with the educational system that they are feel uncomfortable in these settings, are aware of being "talked down to" by teachers and administrators, and are wary that their children will be treated fairly regardless of their advocacy.

Deficit thinking is particularly destructive in that it overlooks many of the structural inequities in schools and in social systems more generally that set minoritized students up to fail. While the answer is not to simply ignore differences in academic achievement, it is critical for teachers to challenge assumptions and stereotypes about students based on race and class while seeking to dismantle systemic inequities that hold these students back. One particularly potent strategy for challenging deficit thinking is culturally relevant pedagogy, wherein teachers try to bring students "funds of knowledge" (Gonzalez et al., 2005) into the curriculum. Funds of knowledge represent a broad array of knowledge that students possess and bring to school with them drawn from their lived experiences, including from their families and culture. As Rios-Aguilar et al. (2011, p. 170) suggest: "Perhaps one of the greatest strengths of the framework of funds of knowledge is that it highlights and values the resources embedded in students, families, and communities, thus countering deficit perspectives." There is a significant body of research demonstrating that when students see themselves and their cultural assets represented in the curriculum, they do better in all aspects of school.

Culturally relevant pedagogy is one method of expanding and diversifying the content of the curriculum, while strategically aligning it to real issues that impact students' lives. Many if not most teacher education programs now emphasize the importance of culturally relevant pedagogy and seek to assist candidates in creating a more diverse and inclusive curriculum. At its best culturally relevant pedagogy involves not only changing the curriculum, but repositioning students to be more engaged in their own learning. As Ladson-Billings (2006, p. 483) describes it, rather than serving to "exoticize" or "other" diverse students, culturally relevant pedagogy is designed to "problematize teaching and encourage teachers to ask about the nature of the student teacher relationship, the curriculum, schooling, and society."

Unfortunately, however, research suggests that just exposing teacher candidates to culturally relevant pedagogy is not necessarily enough to overcome deficit thinking. According to a 2017 study conducted by Sleeter (2017, p. 156) after surveying 1,275 teachers 95% indicated that they were familiar with the concept of culturally responsive pedagogy, with many teachers noting that they learned about it in their teacher education programs. However, in that same study, when asked how they interpreted the low achievement of their students, teachers "most often selected factors related to the students or their homes: attendance and participation (81%), poverty (79%), student motivation (66%), families and communities (52%), and students' home language (30%)." As Sleeter (2017, pp. 156–157) concludes: "What most teachers had learned about culturally responsive pedagogy was not sufficiently potent to disrupt deficit theorizing about students, particularly in schools under pressure to raise student test scores."

So, the questions remain: How do teachers learn about and recognize students' full funds of knowledge, especially those that are not immediately obvious? How do teachers incorporate students' assets into their framing and labeling of students, as well as their expectations for student achievement? How do teachers bridge culturally relevant pedagogy in "theory" with actual meaningful classroom practice that impacts more than just surface level changes in the curriculum without repositioning students?

The activity in this chapter is based on Tara Yosso's iconic 2005 article "Whose Culture Has Capital? A Critical Race Theory Discussion of Community Cultural Wealth." Seeking to challenge the deficit models that define communities of color, Yosso uses critical race theory (CRT) to identify six different and unique forms of "capital wealth," including: *aspirational, navigational, social, familiar, linguistic*, and *resistant* capital. Navigational capital, for example, refers to students' skills and abilities to navigate social institutions. Yosso further explains that students' navigational capital empowers them to maneuver within unsupportive or hostile environments, such as spaces that are not designed for, or welcoming to, people of color. Likewise, *linguistic* capital frames students' ability to communicate in different languages including code-switching and translating, as an asset rather than a deficit. According to Yosso: "This CRT approach to education involves a commitment to develop schools that acknowledge the multiple strengths of Communities of Color in order to serve a larger purpose of struggle toward social and racial justice."

STRATEGY: MAKE A COLLAGE
OF COMMUNITY CULTURAL WEALTH

Using Yosso's six forms of capital (see table 2.1), consider concrete examples of how this capital has been actualized in your own life. Then, create a personal "collage" that represents each of these kinds of cultural capital. You should also feel free to add additional kinds of capital that are not on this list. Also, the term "collage" is defined very loosely, as you are encouraged to use any markers you choose: from family photos, videos, illustrations, advertisements, poems, tapestries, recipes, diaries, and folk tales, to actual spoken word performances, dances, recreations or demonstrations. Just make sure that it is in a format that can be shared with others.

CRITICAL QUESTIONS FOR REFLECTION AND DISCUSSION

- While making your collage, which categories were the hardest to work with?
- If you shared collages with other candidates, what surprised you the most about the reaction to your own collage or your experience of others'?
- In what ways do these different kinds of cultural capital get *acknowledged* or *rewarded* in educational contexts?

Table 2.1. Yosso's Six Forms of Capital

Capital Definition	Examples
Aspirational Capital is the ability to maintain hopes and dreams for the future, even in the face of real and perceived barriers.	family sayings about resilience, "not giving up" or "lifting as you climb," the impact of role models and mentors in shaping goals, overcoming drug addiction, and successfully transitioning out of prison
Linguistic Capital is composed of the intellectual and social skills attained through communication experiences in more than one language and/or style.	bilingualism, translating for parents or family members, code-switching, and signing
Familial Capital is the cultural knowledge nurtured among *familia* (kin) that carry a sense of community history, memory, and cultural intuition.	oral histories, recipes, photographs, maps, songs, bedtime stories, holiday celebrations, knowledge about farming or sewing, methods for saving money, family health, and healing remedies
Social Capital contains networks of people and community resources that provide both instrumental and emotional support to navigate through society's institutions.	job contacts, community center events, school alumni gatherings, military units, access to legal assistance, and financial aid
Navigational Capital is composed of the skills of maneuvering through social institutions, especially those not created with communities of color in mind.	learning how to act when you get pulled over by the police if you are a person of color, when to make direct eye contact with a person in power, how to get a job that requires a certain dress code, and going into a profession that is atypical for your gender or national origin
Resistant Capital contains the knowledge and skills fostered through oppositional behavior that challenges inequality and is grounded in a legacy of resistance to subordination.	opposing beauty norms or gender binaries, resisting attempts to make English one's dominant language, and refusing to comply with racist policies and practices

- In what ways are they ignored, marginalized and/or dismissed?
- How can we become more cognizant of our students' diverse cultural capital, and create classrooms where they are able to use their capital to their individual advantage?
- How can utilizing these different kinds of capital enrich the entire classroom/co-learning experience?
- While making your collage, which categories of capital were the hardest to identify or represent?
- As you think of your own education, in what ways have these different kinds of cultural capital been acknowledged or rewarded in educational

Sample Collage.

contexts? In what ways have they been ignored, marginalized and/or denigrated?

- Reflect on the process of representing your cultural wealth in diverse mediums (visual, written, oral) and of making a collage. How did this contrast to other "autobiographical" assignments in your education?

QUESTIONS FOR CLASSROOM DISCUSSION

After candidates create these collages, they should share them with (or "perform" them for) the rest of the class and reflect on the following:

- What surprised you the most about the reaction to your own collage, or your experience of others' collages?
- What were some of the additional categories of capital wealth that candidates in your class identified?
- How can we become more cognizant of our students' diverse cultural capital, and create classrooms where they are able to use their capital to their individual advantage?
- How can utilizing these different kinds of capital enrich the entire classroom/co-learning experience?
- What is the potential impact of using an asset-based framework for assessing students rather than a deficit-based framework?

TRANSGRESSIVE VOICES

In the following excerpts from weekly course journals, candidates reflect on the ways that their students and their parents are subject to deficit thinking by teachers and administrators at their schools. In the first excerpt, Cary recalls students in her school being told they were "dumb," "an asshole," or would end up "on the corner." In the second excerpt, Lisa describes an incident wherein a teacher at her school described a parent as "typical white trash," believing that "because she didn't have any money that equating her to an inanimate object of little monetary value (trash) was acceptable." In the third excerpt, Marcus laments how some of his favorite students are labeled student "lazy" or "disruptive" by pervious teachers, leading current teachers to treat them like that "from the get-go." In the last excerpt, Dominic lists some of the negative feedback his students have received from teachers which they believe belittles them, such as "What's wrong with you?" and "What are you guys going to do when you get to college? You are going to fail." In all of these narratives, the candidates note that students and parents are aware of these negative labels, that they "feel it and interpret it" and in, many cases, it "reinforces the message that they are not worthy or capable of an education." This, in turn, causes them to both internalize the feedback and subsequently disengage from school.

Cary

I have had multiple students tell me that I was the only teacher that cares about them. I wonder what actions or words translate to caring for our kids.

Each of my students reported a negative experience with a teacher, relating to the idea of low teacher expectations or underlying stereotypes. Students could easily recall times teachers called them dumb, an asshole, or told them their options are jail or a graveyard. It is not just a few interactions like these that affect the students' ability to identify with education. Rather, they have been consistently exposed to teachers who have low expectation or appear not to care about them. Furthermore, three out of the four students reported that a teacher has told them that if they did not stay in that school, they would be on the corner. Although these comments are mostly likely meant to be a wake-up call, they come across as low expectations from teachers. Teachers are meant to be a support system. It is unfortunate that they, probably unintentionally, push students away from academics. Oftentimes our means of discipline, such as sending them out of the classroom, reinforces the message that they are not worthy or capable of an education.

Lisa

A parent in my school was not present but was being discussed by three of the student's former teachers (including myself) and the counselor. One of my co-workers called the students' mother "typical white trash." My co-worker comes from a suburban area outside Philadelphia that certainly has access to more resources and money than do the neighborhoods in which my students reside. The statement was classist in that, because the parent did not have money, equating her to an inanimate object of little monetary value (trash) was acceptable. When I attempted to address this with my co-worker, she told me I could not understand her use of this word because I was not from the Philadelphia area. I felt belittled by this statement, as if the impact the comment had on me was not valid because I was born outside Philadelphia. Thinking outside of how I felt, I had questions about what this means for the culture of my school, considering this teacher felt justified in making this statement in front of other staff members. More immediately, however, I was considering how this type of mindset affects how teachers interact with other families and if I perpetuate any of these ideas in my own language as an educator. The week following the incidents, we had a parent meeting with a current student's mother. In this meeting she explicitly called out the teacher who had called another student's mother "trash." She said she does not like the way in which the teacher speaks to her son or to her as a parent. This confirmed my belief that the biases we hold as teachers can be felt by both families and students.

Marcus

At the beginning of the school year, teachers pass down information about students to next year's teachers, and I knew specific things about specific students before I even met them. Teachers label them as "lazy" or "disruptive" or "on task" or "motivated" and then I truly believe they treat them as such from the get-go. If we have students who are "disruptive" or "lazy" we should be trying to figure out *why* they are this way, instead of figuring out which punishment will change them to be better behaved. I try very hard not to let these labels affect me before I even get to know a student. One of this year's so called "bad" students is my favorite. With me, he participates in class, gets his work done, and is respectful, is kind, is helpful, and we have created a very strong relationship. Other teachers don't all see him this way, though, and I think it's because they had a preconceived notion of him before he even began 12th grade. This makes me upset, especially because students can definitely feel it and interpret it. They know when a teacher doesn't like them or doesn't think highly of them, and I believe this absolutely affects their actions. If a student doesn't think a teacher sees potential in him/her, why would that student be motivated to do well in class?

Dominic

Students were asked to speak about a time a teacher made them feel bad about their intellect or academic ability and to provide concrete examples of words or phrases the teacher used to make them feel that way. The answers to these questions were heartbreaking. Every student was able to provide an example of a time this either happened to them or a time they saw it happen to someone else, with one student explaining that these negative interactions "can hurt somebody's ego, especially when we're about to go to college." The following are a list of phrases students have heard teachers say that have belittled them:

- "What is wrong with you? Why don't you get this? It's easy math."
- "You're being brats."
- "You guys don't do anything. What are you going to do when you get to college? You guys are going to fail."
- "You really don't get it? It's easy. Do I really have to stay after school?"
- "I just went over this shit. Really?"
- "Ugh."
- "Do you even know what this word means?"

After providing examples, a student in Group 4 further explained, "The worst things that you can hear you're already telling yourself, so you don't want to hear it from somebody else." If teachers are supposed to be the role models and adults students look up to for support and encouragement, what message are they sending those students if comments like the ones above are coming from their mouths?

Chapter Three

Gap Gazing—Who Are *Those* Kids?

Strategy: Critical Discourse Analysis

"Educational researchers, practitioners and policymakers have been so meshed in the work to remedy the achievement gap, that not enough attention has been given to how assumption-laden Discourse and subsequent practices of contemporary schooling have left millions of students, teachers, and schools labeled, categorized, and scrutinized in recent years."—Cary, 2014, p. 444

Key Concepts

Gap Gazing and Critical Discourse Analysis

Goals

- To unpack the buzzwords and assumptions behind key educational discourses such as "the achievement gap," "at-risk students," "proficiency," and "accountability."
- To understand how and why certain ideologies about student achievement (or lack of achievement) are constructed and enduring.
- To consider how different educational discourses can lead to particular educational stances and practices that not only impact the present but serve to shape the future of educational policy and practice.

ABOUT "GAP GAZING" AND CRITICAL DISCOURSE ANALYSIS

As discussed in chapter's 1 and 2, the language most commonly used to describe failing students focuses on "the achievement gap." The reasons for the achievement gap run the gamut from theories about *The Bell Curve* (Herrnstein & Murray, 1994) that suggests that certain racial groups are genetically less intelligent than others, to *grit* (Duckworth, 2016) wherein certain students are perceived to have more internal motivation and perseverance than others, to the "model minority" where certain cultures are thought to value education more than others. The achievement gap has been a persistent discourse in education since the publication of *A Nation at Risk* and the subsequent educational policy embedded in *No Child Left Behind* or Every Student Succeeds Act (ESSA). In terms of pure data points, the achievement gap represents differential test scores, high school retention and college acceptance rates between middle- and upper-class White students and working- or lower-class students of color. Critics of the achievement gap have argued that these gaps—while real—are not a result of individual intelligence or cultural work ethics. Rather, patterns of difference in student achievement can be attributed to a wide range of gaps, including: the teacher quality and training gap, the challenging curriculum gap, the school funding gap, the wealth and income gap, the health care gap, and the school integration gap, among many others (Carey, 2014, p. 447).

Put more simply, it is unrealistic to expect students to perform equally well in school when schools themselves are so unequal, and when so many students lack basic necessities such as food and health care. As a result, many educators have begun to talk about opportunity gaps, and more recently, the educational debt (Ladson-Billings, 2006), which is suggestive of decades of systemic discrimination, racism, and oppression that have literally held back students of color from reaching their full potential and demand reparation. Milner (2013) further suggests that the achievement gap discourse might also contribute to the very problems they seek to solve by redirecting attention away from systemic inequities and placing blame directly on students and their families.

The related concept of "gap gazing" began with the work of Gutiérrez (2008) and Gutiérrez and Dixon-Román (2011), who suggest that rather than getting at the root of these gaps and subsequently changing the circumstances that create them, many educators are still simply trying to explain or justify them. According to Gutiérrez (p. 358): "At their most extreme, achievement gap studies offer little more than static pictures of inequities in schools . . . knowing that the gap has widened and narrowed over the past two decades has provided little direction for eliminating the gap." Like Milner, Gutiérrez further suggests that "gap gazing" serves to perpetuate the myth that educational equity is a purely technical problem that can be solved by individual teachers and "best" teaching practices rather the need to invest in larger social systems that impact educational inequity.

Yet, how can we expect students with vastly inferior resources and cultural capital to do as well as those with so many more opportunities? Put more bluntly: How can we expect students in schools without computers, working bathrooms, school counselors, functioning libraries, certified teachers, and up-to-date textbooks to compete with schools with science and computer labs, swimming pools, and study abroad opportunities? How can we compare students who regularly go to over-crowded classes with substitute teachers who know nothing about them, to students who get to learn in small groups with experienced teachers and personal advisors?

Because these structural inequalities between opportunities are not random but follow closely historic inequalities based on race and class, many educators have begun to believe that even the term "opportunity gap," is not politicized enough. Gloria Ladson-Billings (2006, p. 5), for example, has famously talked about the *education debt*: "I am arguing that the historical, economic, sociopolitical, and moral decisions and policies that characterize our society have created an educational debt." The language of an "educational debt" is vitally different from that of either achievement gap or opportunity gap because it implies that these gaps are neither accidental nor arbitrary. Ladson-Billings reminds us that America has a long history of morally rationalizing why certain groups are more deserving than others, economically hoarding assets and capital, and politically disenfranchising people who threaten the status quo of power, privilege, and advantage.

The strategy in this chapter is designed to help candidates look more closely at discourses such as the achievement gap and identify the ideologies about student achievement inherent in those discourses. The strategy directs candidates to use Critical Discourse Analysis (CDA), a theory which views language as a form of social practice. According to Mullet (2018), CDA is premised on the idea that how we use language is intentional and purposeful, regardless of whether we these choices are conscious or not. Close readings of words and phrases used to describe education uncover profound and enduring discourses about race, equity and achievement. When engaging in CDA, however, it is important to remember that, as Apple (2014, p. 20) suggests: "The first thing to ask about an ideology is not what is false about it but what is true. What are its connections to lived experiences? Ideologies, properly conceived, do not dupe people. To be effective, they must connect to real problems, real experiences."

EXAMPLES OF CRITICAL DISCOURSE ANALYSIS

The examples in this section are adapted from my previous book *Embracing Risk in Urban Education*.

Example #1: "All About Choice"

The following remarks were made to students on their first day of school at a charter school by the school's co-founder. "This school is all about choice. . . . See that back door? See any locks on it? Is this a prison? Am I forcing you to be here? . . . If you cannot live by our rules, if you cannot adapt to this place, I can show you the back door." Reading this passage carefully, you can see that the founder suggests that students who disagree with the rules should have to leave, and further, should leave through the *back* door. Why shouldn't they be allowed to leave through the front door? What does the *back* door convey to students about their actual freedom of choice? Also, the language here suggests that the only rules that are important are those made by the school itself (e.g. "our rules"), and that students have no choice but to "adapt" to them or leave. While it is certainly within the school's rights to create and enforce their own rules, this particular "Discourse" reflects an ideology of authoritarianism rather than being "all about choice."

Example #2: "Those Kids"

Arne Duncan, the secretary of education under President Obama, once said: "Closing underperforming schools may seem like a surrender, but in some cases it's the only responsible thing to do. It instantly improves the learning conditions for those kids and brings a failing school to a swift and thorough conclusion." There is a lot to unpack here. First, there is the use of the term "underperforming" which suggests a common definition of/agreement with what that means. For example, while there are certainly quantifiable differences in schools' standardized test scores, this does not mean that the school is not excelling or serving students well in other ways. Next, the use of the word "surrender" suggests that education is a kind of war or game and that schools are soldiers or pawns rather than humanistic institutions. Additionally, the use of the term "those kids" suggests that a particular kind of student attends underperforming schools and that "those kids" are somehow different from "our kids." Lastly, when Duncan talks about bringing schools to a "swift and thorough conclusion" he seems to be comparing schools to a kind of novel or perhaps legal trial. In reality, closing a school has vast and significant consequences that are not "swift" and do not simply "conclude" when the building shuts down. In addition to being places where many students have developed trusting relationships with teachers and look to staff as role models and mentors, public schools are places where students get food, which families look to for childcare, and where community citizens go to vote. Lastly this quote implies that "those kids" have other schools to choose from, which is often not the case.

Example #3: "Teach a Rock to Read"

An urban superintendent once remarked to the teachers in her district: "What we need are teachers who don't make excuses. I don't want to hear about bureaucracy. We have always had bureaucracies. We are looking for people who say, 'I can teach a rock to read.' If this is not the right place for you, then you should find another place to go." Similar to the first example, the implication here is that teachers have complete freedom of choice, and if they aren't happy at one school, they can simply transfer to another. In reality most urban school systems have very strict policies about assigning teachers to specific schools and the conditions under which they are allowed to choose where (and what) they teach. Secondly, the use of the "excuses" suggests that teachers who are struggling with student achievement are simply not trying hard enough or working hard enough, a.k.a. they are looking for "excuses" rather than increased resources and support. This completely ignores many of the structural inequities that teachers have no control over. Lastly, the idea that the district is looking for people who say they can "teach a rock to read" suggests that students who attend schools in this district (which is largely minority, low-income students) have the intelligence of a "rock."

- Identify passages about education in diverse contexts, such as: newspapers and magazines, popular and academic journals, policy briefs and political speeches, school websites and newsletters, etc. Look for passages that use educational buzzwords such as "at-risk," "grit," 'intelligent," "under-achieving," "urban," "underserved," "minority," or "proficiency."
- Use CDA to identify and unpack what these particular words and phrases signify and symbolize in the context they are used, and the underlying ideologies. Pay close attention to the wording and phrasing, including words such as "our students" or "those kids" or "urban students." What symbolic words or phrases are used to represent particular groups of students without naming them? How do these phrases "other" certain groups of children while validating other groups of children? Pay attention to the metaphors used to describe education and schools, such as prisons or war games. Pay close attention to "assumptions" that may or may not be true. For example, that swiftly closing underperforming schools is the best course of action, or that teachers who are struggling are looking for "excuses."
- What are some of the common/repeating assumptions across the different examples you found?
- (Why) do you think these Discourses are effective?
- Practice rewriting the passages, substituting words (such as opportunity gap for achievement gap, or "our kids" for "those kids") and consider how

using different words or rephrasing these passages would change their meaning and/or alter strategic actions associated with them.

CRITICAL REFLECTION QUESTIONS

- What are the range of ways that we define student achievement and explain differences in student achievement?
- Likewise, what are some of the common/repeating buzzwords or assumptions about student achievement across the different examples you found? What "fears" do they tap into?
- What kinds of "actions" underlie these ideologies and assumptions? What do they suggest about individuals, systems, and school reform mandates more generally?
- How might closer attention to the cultural and symbolic underpinnings of these terms urge educational stakeholders to reshape the discourse of public school reform?

QUESTIONS FOR CLASSROOM DISCUSSION

- In listening to your classmates CDA did you find that you highlighted any of the same words and phrases? If so, was there symmetry in how you analyzed their meaning and impact? If you disagreed, was there anything about the larger context the words or phrases were embedded in that changed the meaning?
- Ask your classmates to "rewrite" some of the passages you found and compare their revisions to yours.

Passage/ Source	Key Words	Implicit/ Explicit Associations	Effectiveness	Rewrite

Strategy: Critical Discourse Analysis

TRANSGRESSIVE VOICES

The following excerpts from candidates' weekly course journals emphasize the impact of the language and Discourses we use to describe education and schooling on students and teachers. In the first excerpt Tisha describes how in her school, which is made up of almost entirely low-income African American students, teachers use metaphors of "monsters" to labels first grade students. Specifically, students are called "demons, vampires and terrorists." This discourse is significant in light of current statistics about Black males who are immediately suspect when walking in stores and public places that are predominantly White and are disproportionally arrested and murdered by police officers under the assumption that they are inherently "dangerous."

In the second excerpt, Liza reflects on her school's use of language such as "access to a quality education" in its mission statement when in fact that culture of the school is more one of "saving" poor minority students. Liza believes that practitioners at the school actually have extremely low expectations for these students but use "coded language" either to insulate people against conversations about race and class and privilege that are sometimes painful or in the name of "protecting" students and teachers from harsh realities. Liza suggests that teachers—including herself—use synonyms that appear to be less provocative which in turn leads many teachers to adopt a "race-blind" or "color-blind" discourse that reinforces ideas of meritocracy and ignores structural and systemic racism. Liza also reflects on the ways that teachers who work in these schools are considered to be "saviors," implying that teachers who work with minoritized and underserved students need to be "saved" rather than empowered. In the last excerpt Rosa reconsiders her use of the term "reach"—as in, "how do I reach my students?—wondering if this word is reflective of racial and socioeconomic differences and distances between herself and her students.

Tisha

As a new teacher, I experienced first-hand the warning about certain students and the list of labels to describe young children. A teacher at my school went through my roll list describing students she had the year before as "demons, vampires, and terrorists." Demons were students who didn't follow the teacher's orders. Vampires were students who bit other students. Terrorists were students who got into fights with other students. I was stressing about all of the things they could do wrong, and I entered into the classroom with a reactive mindset. Based on what we hear, educators decide how to interact, seat, teach, and monitor students. Many of these labels are not directly communicated to students, however they know there is an overall negative view of them. I message things about my students because they are heavily labeled and their academic capabilities are not taken seriously. Even when I interact with them, I need to operate with this reality in mind. As I continue to struggle, I am consistently reminded by my class that they are not the "crazy" bunch I saw them as initially but a group of kids who have already been so neglected and marginalized at a very young, fragile age. A majority of my students are labeled as struggling learners instead of learners with unique styles. Many people overlook their intellect and the thought-provoking discussion and questions they partake in because they are seen as lacking something. They carry labels and stigma everywhere they go, and they struggle to find a place in an educational framework that does not care to invest in them.

Liza

I learned about a new consequence of privilege. What others have already deemed as "saviors," I now think of "those who pave the path to hell with good intentions." I know, in my head, what the savior complex means by this point in my life. I can read and regurgitate it. There are unspoken benefits to being a savior. Saviors, like me, speak the language. They know how to navigate the language, seemingly applying the appropriate language to different audiences. Saviors transition between using "people of color" versus "black" versus "African American" versus "black and brown." They know in which circles they should say "poor" because it's more charged than "free and reduced lunch." I know that when I say "hard to staff school" I mean a school where students fight and are absent and talk back to teachers, but I don't say this. Sometimes I will say "schools with high safety incidences." It has not been until this semester that I've truly witnessed the way in which I use evasive language when it suits me, when it suits my work, and my audience. Why do people use coded language in talk about urban education? Is it used to protect students? Teachers? Or to view mindsets and truths that are hard to talk about? Is there a currency to coded language? What would happen if privileged people unveiled the language we use to talk about students of color? Students who are poor? What conditions would people need to do this unveiling?

In both schools I worked at, the vision and mission statement used the word "access." One names "access to a quality education" as its mission, and the other names "access to a great school" as its mission. Both name children as the primary recipient of their work. As I applied to both organizations, these particular words clued me in to the types of work with which these organizations engaged. I assumed that because these mission statements aligned so closely to the schools that I worked in for the previous five years that the organizations would believe in being antiracist practitioners. . . . To be blunt, and also honest, the work that was and is being done in the name of these organizations' missions is unquestioned because they have learned how to capitalize on the currency, that is the language they use to describe their work. The work of these people and organizations is glorified because they built to help children get access to a good education, their intentions are assumed good. The product of organizations, like these, is not assessed because the language they use to describe their work reads as such: "we help black and brown and poor kids and at least we're doing something because something is better than nothing." If this is indeed true, there are racist and classist undertones imbedded in this interpretation and it is steeped in white privilege. Might coded language be used to insulate people against conversations about race and class and privilege that are sometimes painful?

Rosa

I wrote about what changes I might need to make to 'reach' my students. It may be overanalyzing, but I can't help but wonder about my selection of the word 'reach.' Reach creates a distance between them and I. It implies that I must strain against myself to get to them, as it is not within a natural distance. I wonder if I had been talking about students who looked like me or came from a similar background as me, if I would have used a more academically focused word like understand or comprehend.

Chapter Four

Smartness as Cultural Practice

Strategy: Figuring the Worlds and Artifacts of Smartness

"The figured world of smartness is located within us, not as a biological capacity but, instead, as a cultural practice we use to invest meaning in others and ourselves. If we fail to pay attention to how smartness operates in schools and within larger society, we miss a critical opportunity to reimagine and reinterpret smartness, particularly for low-income students and students of color. We also miss the opportunity to explore how we perpetuate it ourselves. We must see smartness as a tool of control and social positioning. Only then can we begin to disrupt smartness in everyday schooling practices, empowering students to frame and author their lives."—Beth Hatt, 2012, p. 457

Key Concepts

Smartness as Cultural Practice, Classroom Artifacts, and Surveillance

Goals

- Distinguish between student intelligence/learning potential and the ideologies of compliance and assimilation.
- Understand they ways that "smartness" is used as "a mechanism of control across race and class lines" (Hatt, 2012).
- Unpack the "the classroom artifacts" that are used to create smartness as a "collective event" (Hatt, 2012).
- Consider how teachers unconsciously and consciously use surveillance to "notice" the actions of certain students over others.
- Reflect on how the systems we use to discipline students may end up silencing and disengaging them.

ABOUT "SMARTNESS AS CULTURAL PRACTICE," CLASSROOM ARTIFACTS, AND SURVEILLANCE

Debates about how to identify, measure and reward "smartness" have always been fundamental to public education. Public schools have long been places where students are sorted and "tracked" according to their perceived ability and potential. When it comes to urban education, these debates have been particularly volatile, as statistics show that certain groups of students in urban schools are perpetually "at-risk" for failing. Researchers, administrators, funders and policymakers continually call attention to lower standardized test scores and higher dropout rates of students who come from low-income and minority backgrounds. How to understand—and address—this disjunction is continually evolving. As previously discussed, most commonly the language used to describe failing students focuses on "the achievement gap."

In her ethnographic study, titled "Smartness as Cultural Practice in Schools," Beth Hatt suggests another vantage point for looking at student achievement. Hatt believes that culturally prescribed standards of student behavior and compliance in the classroom becomes inherently tied to issues of individual students' "smartness," which then become tied to issues of privilege and achievement. According to Hatt, smartness is "not just an ideology or belief but an actual practice: more verb than noun." Hatt (2012, pp. 439–442) argues that "smartness or implicit intelligence is something done to others as social positioning," and that schools use smartness as a "mechanism of control and social positioning along racial and class lines."

Hatt spent one year studying a Kindergarten classroom in the southeastern United States using the guiding research questions: Who has power? How is it enacted? What actions in the classroom constitute "privilege" and how is privilege negotiated? Her research uncovered a direct connection between the construction of "smartness," and the distribution of power. Looking closely at daily classroom practices such as the traffic spotlight, Hatt (2012) was able to demonstrate concrete ways in which defining and publicly identifying smartness became a tool for maintaining power and limiting who has access to power. The traffic spotlight is an extremely common practice in elementary education whereby the front of the classroom includes a large visual traffic spotlight, and each student has a cardboard car that moves between green, yellow and red depending upon their minute-to-minute behavior. During the day, where their car rests, determines what privileges students are entitled to (e.g., getting their snacks or nap blankets before other students). At the end of the day, whatever color students are on is reported and sent home to their parents, thus defining the students' actions in one final, quantifiable code. The traffic spotlight thus became a "cultural artifact" that defined the "figured worlds" of the classroom and hierarchically positioned students within it.

While this may on the surface appear to simply be a way of helping students to self-regulate and modify disruptive behaviors, over time Hatt observed the way the teacher conflated being compliant and being "smart." Students who raised their hand, or sat quietly on the rug, were not only told they were making "good choices," but that they were smart—or even "brilliant" for doing so. Students who had trouble obeying the classroom rules, on the other hand, were publicly admonished and told that were not smart. Hatt further observed that many times the teacher unevenly noticed and reprimanded students, discovering that "certain students were asked to move their cars faster while other students were better at breaking rules and getting caught." Hatt found, for example, that African American male students were repeatedly the first to get into trouble and received the harshest admonishments. By contrast, Hatt observed White boys from middle class families exhibiting the same behavior with no consequences. Hatt calls this concept "surveillance" as it suggests that teachers see only what they are looking for. Hatt concludes that smartness became a "collective event" in which students were positioned against each other in order to justify and reify power hierarchies based on race and class. According to Hatt (2012, p. 452):

> Students entering kindergarten do not learn an innocent, benign concept of smartness, but a concept used to teach them their status within the classroom and larger society, whether school is a place they fit, and what privileges they deserve. . . . This concept was actively, purposefully used to teach students about themselves. In conjunction with teachers, students learned who was and was not smart, the privileges that went along with being smart, and whether they were smart themselves.

The activity in this chapter seeks to help candidates become more aware of the use of smartness as cultural practice, and to further consider the ways that smartness is constructed along the lines of compliance and culturally dominant expectations for student behavior.

STRATEGY

1. Go to YouTube and search for terms such as "Kindergarten Teacher + Classroom Management." [If you teach a different grade and want to look specifically at that grade that is ok too, however, it is important to understand how "smartness" is "figured" in children's earliest school experiences.]
2. You will find many videos from all across the country, of various lengths, with teachers of different genders and races, and that take

place in schools ranging from public to charter to private. Look for videos which are "homemade" meaning that teachers filmed themselves for the purposes of sharing with other teachers rather than professionally produced by teaching training organizations. Teachers tend to be less "self-conscious" and less scripted in this format.

3. Watch at least four different videos. For each video, keep track of each video using the tracking/observation chart on the two following pages.

CRITICAL REFLECTION QUESTIONS

- What common themes and differences did you see across the four videos? Consider the actual management strategies and techniques teachers used to keep students compliant, as well as the different discourses about smartness.
- Who had the most power and how was this made visible in the different videos? What actions were associated with students being given praise or privilege?
- To what extent could you tie discourses about smartness to issues of race, class, gender, language, (dis)ability, age, and other student characteristics and identities?

FOR CLASSROOM DISCUSSION

Share a video that you watched with a classmate and have them fill-out a blank tracking/observation chart. What were the differences and similarities in your observations and analysis? Where did you agree or disagree? If you disagreed, discuss your viewpoints and perhaps watch the video again together.

TRANSGRESSIVE VOICES

The following excerpts from candidates' weekly course journals support Hatt's observations that "smartness" can be a constructed ideology that is tied to student compliance rather than academic achievement, prowess, or engagement. These excerpts also illustrate how classroom management techniques designed to regulate student behavior can have the opposite effect causing some students to act out, feel "othered" or even feel afraid. In the first excerpt, Rashi echoes much of Hatt's original findings when she asks her students what students they think are the smartest in the classroom. One hundred percent of students picked the most "compliant" girl in the room. In the second excerpt Lilianna also asks her students directly how they feel when they are forced to move their car on the centrally positioned classroom

Table 4.1.   Video Tracking/Observation Chart

	#1	#2	#3	#4
Context of Video: School Site/Demographics, Classroom Grade, Teacher's Race/Gender				
Purpose of Video: In the Introduction to the video what does the teacher say is their purpose in making it and what essential questions or problems they are going to address over the course of the video.				
Management Techniques Covered: What are the different classroom techniques described in the video? What are their specific purposes? What does the teacher call them?				
Smartness: What do you notice about the way "smartness" is framed or defined in the video? What in the teacher's Discourse is suggestive of how s/he decides which students are "smart"?				
Self-Control: What do you notice about the way "self-control" is framed or defined in the video? How heavily does the teacher emphasize the importance of students exercising self-control? What in the teacher's Discourse is suggestive of how self-control is connected to smartness?				

	#1	#2	#3	#4
Obedience: What do you notice about the way "obedience" is framed or defined in the video? How heavily does the teacher emphasize the importance of students doing what they are told in the exact manner that the teacher prescribes it? What in the teacher's Discourse is suggestive of how obedience is connected to self-control and/or smartness?				
Choices: What do you notice about the way (good or bad) "choices" are framed or defined in the video? How heavily does the teacher emphasize the importance of students making "good" choices? What in the teacher's Discourse is suggestive of how good or bad choices are related to obedience, self-control and/or smartness?				
Surveillance: If the teacher films themself teaching in an actual classroom, what do you notice about the way the teacher "surveils" the students to see which students are exercising self-control, obedience, and making good or bad choices? As you think about which students the teacher pays positive or negative attention to, do you see any patterns related to a students' gender or race?				

traffic light. Lilianna finds that it makes students angry to the point that some even want to "hit themselves," or to "holler." Lilianna concluded that the traffic light, rather than helping her students stay focused and engaged was actually causing them real emotional and traumatic stress.

In the third excerpt, Caspar also asks his students how they feel about having their "clip" moved from one color to another (across a string stretching from one end of the classroom to another) based on their behavior throughout the day. In this case, "blue" is the best color. He finds that students are well aware that blue students are considered "smarter" by teachers when in reality, they know that being on blue is about "folding your hands" and "being good." In the last excerpt Mark reflects on his own practice of "giving demerits for small infractions" and his preconception that that is what a "strict" teacher does. Upon further reflection, however, Mark discovers how this creates a significant divide between him and his students accompanied by a struggle for power, leading Mark to question that difference between having students who are "compliant" and students who are "engaged."

Rashi

Recently in my building, I heard a Kindergarten teacher telling the kids, "If you choose not to stand hips and lips and walk out of line then you must not have a brain." Next, she continues to compliment the students walking in a perfect line by saying, "Wow! This group of scholars over here look like a bunch of smart listeners and they make good choices. I even see a genius who has been perfect all day in line." During the transition in the hall, I am reminded that the students who fail to exude total control are made to feel less than or unintelligent. All of the boys in my sample are convinced that because they are hyper-active or impulsive at times that they are not as smart or capable. When I asked for an example of a smart student, 100% of their responses gave an example of a female student who was mild mannered and followed all of the rules. These extremely compliant students were actually not the smartest in their class but they did receive a lot of praise from teachers. Across the sample, I received an overwhelmingly negative response from the first-grade boys about whether or not they have been labeled as "smart" by anyone at school. Four out of six students stated that they have never been called smart by anyone at school. These students are identified by their teacher's surveys as unteachable or carry labels such as: lazy, clowns, slow, violent, wild, class terror, and/or future robbers of America.

It is evident students have a limited view of the good vs. bad student dichotomy. Those seen as intelligent are very much so constructed by teachers and the consequences faced by those not deemed as "ideal" learners is exclusion from class-wide rewards. In class, half of the students shared the experience where they felt like they never get rewards, such as raffle tickets and good lunch. Student awareness that they are not smart or favored leads to disinvestment in class. What motivation does a student have to behave when they are constantly receiving discouraging messages? Often teachers do not openly say they refuse to teach a student, but the archetype of hyperactive urban Black males in education leads to a student feeling disenfranchised and at odds. Essentially, students and teachers valued different things and defined smartness differently. Many of our students lack the investment they need to be successful, and it is essential for teachers to be innovative about finding ways to motivate and support them. When I asked students what it meant to be good or bad, I became aware of how universal their ideals are. Unfortunately, compliance is tied to intellect and many students have been messaged that being docile and following directions makes you smart. I want to teach empowered voices and not compliant robots.

Lilianna

The traffic light is school-wide that consists of four colors, red, yellow, green, and blue. Students' names are visually represented on the traffic light and each student can move from color to color throughout the day. In the classroom studied, students' names are written on clothespins, which can be moved from color to color. . . . When asked about how they feel when they are moved to yellow or red on the traffic light, four students said that this makes them feel sad and they don't like it. The remaining eleven students said that this makes them feel very sad and they hate it. Some student responses stood out among the others: I don't like it when my light changes, it makes me sad, and it makes me mad, mad, mad, really mad; It makes me want to hit myself; It makes me want to holler when I go on yellow or red. Holler like AHH (student yelled). These negative effects include feelings of violence, anger, and sadness. It appears that many students do not feel safe because of these policies, and in some cases, they make students feel the exact opposite of safe.

The possible negative effects on the students' emotional statuses suggest that these policies are actually hurting students' learning experiences. It is important to remember that the students were very young, between the ages of five and six years old. It is unrealistic to suggest that there are no behavior policies in place in a school, but they do not all have to be negative. There must be some sort of order to get work done in the classroom, but there shouldn't be policies that cause students to feel unsafe. The traffic light has shown to be an extremely negative policy in the classroom, and I do hope to use it as minimally as possible after conducting this research. It is important to remember that children make mistakes, and it is how they fix these mistakes that matters the most.

Caspar

When asked to provide clear labels of how teachers view students, my students all spoke explicitly about behavior, with academic success being a smaller factor in how teachers view and label students. The labels they came up with were the smart and/or hardworking students, the middle students, and the students who misbehaved or didn't understand the material. While no teachers in this study tied the public behavior system to grades, each student focus group stated that blue students [students whose daily clip is on the color blue] are smarter. The following is an excerpt from my field notes:

Q: Are blue students smarter?

A#1: Yes, they work hard.

A#2: No, it's not fair if you say you're smarter. Everyone is smart. If you say you are the only one who's smart, that's mean.

Q: Do you have to be smart to be on blue?

A: No. You can fold your hands. You have to be good.

Q: Is it fair?

A: No

Students were intimately aware of the implications of their behavior, and during the course of the discussion, it came to light that students have the best of intentions. Students try their best in a system that highlights their faults for all to see and makes it difficult to celebrate the little successes like sitting quietly. When blue is made to be unattainable, it marginalizes students for whom school does not come naturally. Blue can become an indicator of students for whom school comes naturally—students who are able to "work the system" to their benefit. Other students tied blue to intelligence. Only after deep scrutiny were students able to distinguish that the color chart is not necessarily tied to academics.

All teachers responded to the survey question "Do you have any issues with the color chart?" Despite the different issues with the color chart, each teacher's qualm painted the public tracker as a distraction. "Students are too focused on the color not necessarily the appropriate behavior," mentioned the second-grade teacher. In my own questionnaire, I responded saying; "Students can become preoccupied with colors instead of learning. The public nature of the tracker can cause melt downs." Ultimately, I found that the color chart does not in and of itself motivate kids. It marginalizes students for whom it labels yellow and red. The color chart codes the language used by teachers and students alike, but the color chart acts as distraction and a source of shaming taking away from learning and positive behavior.

Involved students repeatedly mentioned the rewards and positive recognition. From the data collected, I would recommend that elementary teachers utilizing a public tracker focus heavily on positive reinforcement, behavior narration, and utilize grade-level and developmentally appropriate warning systems and redirections for misbehavior. Students in each grade spoke about unique behavior systems during the focus groups. Each grade level focused on positive behavior and rewards. Many also detailed what would happen to students who misbehaved, and one kindergarten student eloquently said, "They would have to listen. We would help our friends [learn to behave]." Students showed great interest in systems that allowed students to shine during their good choices, and external rewards that optimized on individual and whole group participation.

Mark

At the beginning of the year, I found myself giving out demerits for small infractions, such as the students talking during silent work time or getting out of their seats without asking. This is what I thought being a strict teacher was and I wanted to be viewed as a strict teacher. As time went on, I found this tiresome and a detriment to the kind of culture that I was trying to create in my classroom. My classroom management has improved this year, without a doubt. Stopping my class every few minutes to issue demerits created a negative tone in my classroom, and the infractions did not seem to be decreasing as time went on. It also created a divide. I often felt like the class was the students versus me and sometimes I felt helpless as if the class was taking over. Teachers may call students sweet, nice, committed, motivated, a good student, a pain, energetic, distracted, focused, talkative, well-behaved, quiet, shy, busy, etc. A student is considered to have good behavior if he can sit still, quietly and follow the instructions of the teacher, staying on task. We tell students to have more "self-control." Judging a student's self-control as staying on task and following directions is assuming that the student wants to be doing what the teacher is asking. . . . If students are not well behaved, is it because they want to defy the teacher, or they cannot help it? Is it because they cannot complete the task or are lost? Is it because they are bored or disinterested and are choosing not to do the task? How would the teacher know? So, do teachers want students to be compliant or engaged? How are these different or the same?

Chapter Five

A Mission to Question

Strategy: Flipping School Mission Statements

"Many schools have mission and vision statements. . . . What is painfully, distressingly, and alarmingly true about many of these schools is the proportion of them that draft these well-meaning documents, file them, and never ever return to them again—until it is time to craft some sort of improvement plan. This is only slightly better than those who print these driving statements on banners for all who visit to notice, while their actions are in stark contrast with the values that literally hang over their heads. Vision must live in practice."
—Lehman and Chase, 2015, p. 13

"The principle of co-creation rarely appears in school mission statements."
—Chaltain, 2009, p. 57

Note this chapter is best done in conjunction with chapter 6.

Key Concepts

Identifying School Mission Statements, Vision in Practice, Co-creation, and Inquiry-Based School Missions

Goals

- To identify, unpack, and critically examine school mission statements.
- To consider how closely mission statements are (mis)aligned with school practices and to what extent vision lives in practice.
- To engage in the co-creation of inquiry-based school mission statements.

ABOUT SCHOOL MISSION STATEMENTS

It used to be uncommon for public schools to have a formal, identifiable mission statement. The purpose of school was just assumed to be to acquire knowledge, get good grades, pass tests, advance to the next grade, and eventually go on to college or a trade, etc. This has not necessarily been the case for private schools, as they are not founded with the intent of serving all students and therefore need to market and brand themselves to attract the "right" students, especially since they are potentially competitive with each other. In the age of the Internet, however, even public schools have begun to think more intentionally about their public image and mission. This is especially true as many districts have charter and magnet schools that—while technically public—often still require students to "apply." If you go to the websites of some of these public schools you will see diverse mission statements, such as the following:

- The primary mission of The Academy is to provide our students with a comprehensive academic preparation for the rigors of higher learning.
- Our mission is to provide public school students with a comprehensive educational experience that expands students' knowledge of global issues and prepares them for a lifetime of achievement and participation in local, national and global communities.
- Our neighborhood public school fosters rigorous academics and mindful students in an engaged, diverse, environmentally conscious community.
- We prepare boys for success in college and beyond, using as our foundation a classical Latin education, the positive influence of brotherhood, and rich relationships. We are a community that values and cultivates critical thinking, personal responsibility, emotional intelligence, and character development.
- [Name] provides a college-preparatory learning experience with a focus on individual freedom, critical thinking, and problem solving in an environment that emphasizes the values of community, teamwork, and nonviolence.

A quick scan of these mission statements highlights different goals and values, such as: comprehensive academic preparation, mindful students, college preparatory, critical thinking, personal responsibility, individual freedom, teamwork, nonviolence, emotional intelligence, technological skills, problem-solving skills, and global knowledge, etc. *Of note: all five of these public schools are in the same school district.* Whether or not these schools are intentionally designed to promote these values or achieve these goals, however, is another story. (How) are these mission statements actualized and how are they assessed? It is not uncommon for new teachers to be hired by a school with a stated mission to find a huge gap between the ideals and reality of the school purpose and culture. Moreover, it is important to get past the jargon in mission statements, and really probe what some of these terms mean in practice. For example, is "personal responsibility" the same thing as "individual freedom"? What makes academics "rigorous"? What does it mean to refer to a school as a "community"?

By contrast, the mission statement of the Science Leadership Academy (SLA), a public school in the School District of Philadelphia, reads quite differently from those exemplars above. SLA's mission statement, in fact, begins with a series of questions:

- How do we learn?
- What can we create?
- What does it mean to lead?

The fact that SLA's mission statement is in fact not a statement, *but a series of questions*, does not mean it doesn't have a coherent mission and core values. As a school where inquiry is at the heart of all learning: "SLA is built on the notion that inquiry is the very first step in the process of learning." The series of questions that comprise the beginning of SLA's mission statement are aligned with SLA's commitment to creating a school culture of curiosity and discovery. Students at SLA learn in a project-based environment where the *core values* of inquiry, research, collaboration, presentation, and reflection are emphasized in all classes. As SLA's founding principal, Chris Lehman, and veteran teacher Zac Chase (2015, p. 13) underscore: "Vision must live in practice." The activity in this chapter is a means of reflecting on the alignment between school mission statements and their actual practice. Moreover, by "flipping" these mission statements into questions, candidates are prompted to consider what it would mean to have a mission statement that was open to co-creation and that values student voice and inquiry in defining the mission and culture of the school community.

STRATEGY, PART ONE

Step One: Choose a school to work with. It can be a school that you or a family member attended, a school you are doing clinical practice in, a school that you think you would like to teach in, a school that has a great reputation or, conversely, a poor reputation, or a school that you choose completely at random.

Step Two: Identify if your chosen school has a formal mission statement. If so, copy it verbatim on a piece of paper.

Step Three: If no formal mission statement exists, see if you can piece together and construct an implicit mission statement, drawn from websites, newsletters, annual reports, admissions policies, disciplinary policies, awards given out at graduation, etc. **Note:** You can also include visual documents, such as photos found on the school's website or pictures of displays on classroom and hallway walls.

Step Four: Based on the mission statement you choose, highlight what you believe to be the school's core values, rules, standards, expectations, and aspirations.

Critical Reflection Questions

- What aspects of the school's mission do you agree with? What aspects do you disagree with? What aspects are you unsure about and why?
- What aspects of the mission do you think are the most controversial? Why?
- Is the mission statement clearly aligned to a set of values or practices? For example, is "student achievement" defined only by test scores and graduation rates, or does it include other examples of engagement, learning, growth and leadership?
- Do you think this "mission" fits/serves the needs of the particular students in this school? Why/Why not?
- What aspects do you think the students who attend the school would agree with, or take most issue with? Why? (If possible, consider asking them.)
- What about other teachers, administrators, or parents involved in your school community? If asked, would they be able to identify a shared mission or vision for the school? (If possible, consider asking them.)
- In thinking about your own experience working or spending time in this school (if possible), how closely does the mission statement match the actual culture and values of the school? Cite specific examples of alignment or misalignment. Again: This exercise is best done in concert with the observation assignment in chapter 6.

Table 5.1.   School Mission Statements

School:		
Formal Mission Statement	**Implicit Mission Statement**	**Highlight Core Values**

STRATEGY, PART TWO

Go back to the school explicit mission statement you initially identified. How would you describe this school's formal mission statement in the form of *questions*? For example, if one of the components of the school's mission statement is "teamwork," the corresponding questions might be "What is collaborative inquiry?" or "What is distributed leadership?" or "What can we learn from each other?"

Critical Questions

- What is your perceived impact (if any) of changing the mission statement to a series of questions? How (if at all) does changing a statement to a question change the meaning?
- In addition to those questions that you think are aligned with your school's actual mission statement, what questions would *you* choose, and why do you think they are significant questions to ask? For example, you might want to ask the question: "How can we learn from failure?" or "How can we include more diverse perspectives in our understanding of American history?"

Questions for Classroom Discussion

- Compare your schools to other candidates' schools. Were there common mission statements and core values? Did you flip them into the same questions? If not, what accounts for the differences?
- Find a partner and share your mission statements (as statements and as questions). Working together, co-create new mission statements that better align with what you know about the school.

TRANSGRESSIVE VOICES

The following excerpts from candidates' weekly course journals suggest that many teachers are forced to facilitate school practices that are not aligned with the school's explicit mission. In the first excerpt, Janna considers the language used to describe the neighborhood "turnaround" school she teachers at. Despite language in the mission statement such as "building a community of life-long learners" she observes that most of her students "don't care about school." She attributes this to a lack of student ownership which ultimately leads students to feel "tired," "frustrated" and "annoyed" and wonders what authentic "community building" would be like in her school. In the second excerpt Amy notes that: "Schools have very sophisticated visions and

missions but are not living up to them." Amy points to racial and socioeconomic status as a major factor in why urban schools lack the resources of
their suburban counterparts and laments that for minority students in poor
urban neighborhoods "schools just serve as buildings where children are
being housed for 8 or more hours a day and being taught to follow rules."
Much like Janna, Amy laments the loss of students' critical thinking and love
of learning that is left in the wake of urban education. In the third excerpt
Monica likewise agrees that "even schools who claim to fight for equity"
have a vision statement that is centered around discipline rather than learning, and that in her school they care more about dress codes than whether
students really understand the concepts they are being taught.

Janna

I work at Haydon Charter School, a turnaround middle school in Philadelphia. Haydon boasts a relatively diverse population, comprised of 76%
Black, 15.5% Asian, 5% Hispanic, 2.5% White, and 1.5% other students; all
qualify for free/reduced lunch. In its 4 years as a turnaround school, Haydon
has seen two Principals, three Assistant Principals, and a long roster of teachers. Yet, one consistent element of the school has been its mission statement
of guiding scholars towards independence by "building a community of life-
long learners." Despite this mission, I have often heard students say "I don't
care" or "It doesn't matter" when in reference to their academics, while
teachers and staff lament the lack of ownership students have of their work.
These mindsets seem counterintuitive to Haydon's mission.

Outside of the classroom, my students are enthusiastic about a number of
things, such as relationships, sports, and music. I know that apathy and
disconnection is not just a personality trait, so I am hesitant to deem it as a
simple defense mechanism or learned response. In my attempt to understand
my students' lack of ownership and increase it, I considered my school's role
in perpetuating and eradicating the problem. Ideologically, Haydon vacillates
between a "no-excuses" and "restorative-practice" model, that dictates what
students where and how they should behave but leaves holes in terms of
classroom instruction. This leads to inconsistencies in pedagogy and in practice, with teachers often having to individually modify underdeveloped curriculum and insufficient methods. In addition, regardless of restorative talks,
parent meetings, and extra support, students are often found cutting class or
absent all together, with little to no desire to be a part of the learning community.

My students are very vocal about their exasperations with school, often
complaining that work is boring, teachers are "doing too much," and assignments are pointless. Whenever I hear these complaints, I would prompt my
students to tell me what they expected from the school and their teachers.

Very few of them could specifically articulate their concerns and had clearly never been asked to before. I wondered what my students felt the point of school was, and whether they felt like their classes were meaningful and beneficial for them. If my students felt that school was about them— working with them and for them— would they be more invested in their work and take responsibility for their own academic success? I consider the implications that student mindsets around school will have on their futures. Are these feelings specific to an environment that calls itself a "community of learners" despite a lack of academic unity?

The media portrayal of low class, minority youth as uneducated and uninterested is perpetuated by singular narratives of failing schools serving these communities. In addition, my students are still bombarded with messages that juxtapose white, middle class academic success with minority success in sports, music, and entertainment. The narrative that they are not taught to value education in the same way that their white, middle class counterparts are. They are not internally motivated, so instead, we find ways of externally motivating them through incentive systems that tie a materialistic value to learning. If we can target ways to give students a sense of ownership in their own learning, I believe that students will have a stronger stake hold in their own education and could change the perception and realities of their communities.

When I asked my students to discuss their attitudes towards school and who or what influenced these attitudes, a majority of the students reported feeling either "tired," "annoyed," or "frustrated" with school, with a few students noting that they were "proud" or "passionate." It was interesting that students often put both "proud" and "tired," as highlighted by one student's response: "They give us a lot of work all due at once, but I still find a way to turn it all in." Most of the students felt tired with the school environment as a whole and annoyed at the larger school systems which they felt didn't actually promote learning or "allow them to get work done."

When teachers (and students) view learning not as a fixed goal, but as a constant journey, students are more likely to take responsibility for work in the classroom. Meaningful and intentional curriculum is a cornerstone of student ownership within the classroom. Educators and researchers alike emphasize the importance of making work relevant to students, highlighting pedagogy that creates "real-world" connections for students and brings their culture, lives, and backgrounds into the classroom. What I have personally found is that, for many teachers this translates to tapping into students' interests and using that to create interesting lesson plans. However, the problem that I have come to recognize in this practice is that teachers (particularly novice teachers) often rely on surface level, stereotypic ideas of what their students are interested in, and focus more on making students comfortable than exposing them to what is useful and needed.

If students are not active, responsible participants in the ethos of the learning environment, they are less likely to feel like their work is important. In addition, if students are not able to see success as a combination of ability and effort, students will then resort into self-worth preservation mode so as to protect fragile senses of self-worth. Increasing student ownership allows students to see the *work* behind academic success and creates a bond between student and academics that, ideally, fosters a sense of pride and develops a strong academic identity. I feel that student ownership is integral in any classroom because it goes a step past student engagement (in which students are interested in and active participants in their work) with the goal of helping students to foster an identity— or part of an identity— that includes their academics.

Amy

My opinion of education is beginning to shift because schools have these very sophisticated visions and missions but are not living up to them. Students in urban schools do not have access to the same things as wealthy suburban counterparts, but they are expected to achieve at the same levels. Teachers are deterred away from giving their heart and souls to the education. Teachers not trusted to do the job they believe firmly in are just people taking orders from the boss. Education no longer seems like a priority, but more like something all children need to have in order to be able to check off another thing on their checklist of life. Racial and socioeconomic status plays a vital role on these educational dilemmas. Urban schools are in poor neighborhoods, are poorly funded, populated by minorities, run and operated by inexperienced teachers and leaders. My students are used to teachers leaving them and often feeling frustrated by not being able to invest better in the lives of their students. Schools are now just serving as buildings where children are being housed for 8 or more hours a day and being taught to follow rules. Schools have the power to be places that inspire children to think outside the box, to be critical and analytical thinkers, and develop a love for learning that will get them far in life.

Monica

Even schools who claim to fight for equity many times will make their mission statement one that centers around discipline instead of learning. These "no excuses" schools care about results but not the student's journey to truly understand the information. They want the good test scores so that they can get funding from the government, and it does not matter if the students actually know what is required about the topics. The idea of standardized testing in general perpetuated inequality because the questions on these tests are often racist, ableist, or pertain to a middle-class lifestyle that poorer students would not understand. . . . In some cases, students spend more time learning how to take a test better and make "informed guesses" instead of just learning the curriculum. These types of schools care more if the student is out of dress code instead of if they understand concepts.

Chapter Six

Learning from the Shadows

Strategy: Observing Schools as Living Entities

"In one approach, schools and the individuals who inhabit them are managed like machines, and people are given prepackaged 'solutions' that supersede community input; in the other, people and organizations are seen as complex, living systems, and the inherent creativity and commitment of the people being asked to change is what drives all decisions. . . . If the shared culture of the school I visited was a living thing, what would it look, feel, and act like? If that living thing could talk, what would it say to us? If it could develop, what would it morph into next? What aspects of the culture (good and bad) allow it to thrive? What aspects (good and bad) are hindering its further development?"—Chaltain, 2009, pp. 70 and 49

Note: This activity is best done in conjunction with the observation assignment in chapter 5.

Concepts

School Observation, School Culture, Organizational Dynamics, and Schools as "Living Entities"

Goals

- Learn to observe schools as "living entities" and to understand the ways in which schools, and the communities within them, are complex systems that are dynamic, interactional, constantly changing.
- Understand the role "perspective" and "interaction" play in creating school cultures.

51

- Practice observing schools while paying particular attention to verbal and nonverbal communication and issues of agency and power.

ABOUT SCHOOLS AS LIVING ENTITIES

The history of American school reform is as long as the history of American schools. During the period of 1960–1990, for example, Gibboney (1994, p. 15) counted over seventy-five kinds of reform initiatives that gained some attention or notoriety. The literature on school reform reflects deep disagreements over fundamental questions of *what* needs reforming, *how extensive* reforms should be, *where* reforms should take place, and *why* different reforms are necessary. Exactly whose reform goals are we assessing? What happens when some practitioners attempt a reform while others resist or undermine it? What happens when one reform initiative is replaced by or added to another?

As Tyack and Cuban (1995, p. 82) wryly noted: "Policymakers may 'ignore the pedagogical past,' but teachers and students cannot." These "insiders" are tasked with integrating many different reform mandates, a task that Darling-Hammond (2011) has called the "geological dig." Indeed, one does not have to look hard at the history of American public education to see a picture of multiple, disconnected, and short-lived educational programs and policies, the majority of which fail to make a deep and systemic impact on schools, on teachers' practice, and on students' lives. As Hess (1998, p. 99) noted over two decades ago, "Despite the common belief that reform is the key to shattering the status quo, the truth is that a state of perpetual reform is the status quo." According to Hess (p. 5):

> Not only are districts pursuing an immense number of reforms, they recycle initiatives, constantly modify previous initiatives, and adopt innovative reform A to replace practice B even as another district is adopting B as an innovative reform to practice A.

Relatively recent national reform initiatives such as No Child Left Behind (NCLB), Race to the Top (RTTT), and Common Core State Standards serve as good examples of policies that attempt broad scale, highly regulated changes, but fail to consider the unique context of schools and the personalities and visions of the people who work and reside inside them.

In *American Schools: The Art of Creating a Democratic Learning Community*, Sam Chaltain (2009, p. 55) describes three basic characteristics of living systems: "they constantly change and recreate themselves; they constantly reorganize themselves in unpredictable ways; and they constantly demonstrate their awareness by the way they interact with their environment." Chaltain warns however that: "The symptoms of these factors at work . . . are often ignored or disregarded." This is especially true in American public schools where school reform efforts on a national, state and local scale are both highly prescriptive and seemingly never-ending. In the midst of constantly changing priorities and mandates, it is easy for school administrators and teachers to feel a sense of chaos, frustration, disillusionment, and disengagement.

According to Chaltain (p. 56), one of the reasons that many people resist school reforms or any kind of change is that they do not feel included in the process as "[p]eople only support what they create" and, moreover, that to be invested in change "people need to believe that the change taking place is meaningful." While most school reforms are, in fact, meaningful, the missing step is that their meaning is often not clear to those who must enact the reforms, especially when they consist of mandates which are not realistic and wherein failing to meet the goals lead to punitive measures. Put simply, it is critical that all educational stakeholders—and most centrally teachers—need to be deeply and authentically involved in school reform mandates, or what Chaltain calls "generative complexity." In healthy organizational culture leaders "create the conditions that will support that process of co-creation" (p. 56). As Chaltain concludes, attempts to creative a more inclusive school environment and culture "must therefore begin with the recognition that schools are not machines; they are complex, living systems" (p. 58).

STRATEGY

Step One: Choose a school to work with for this strategy. Ideally it is a school that you familiar with, such as a school you or a family member attended, or a school you are doing clinical practice in. *Note: You may want to consider doing this assignment in pairs as interaction and differences in perspective is a key part of the learning goal.*

Step Two: If this is not a school you already work in, obtain the required permissions to do an observation (60 minutes should be the minimum although ideally you would spend an entire day there). If you already work in the school, obtain permissions and block out time to observe different parts of the schools and times of day (such as gym/lunch/recess, a classroom with younger or older students than those you work with, or a classroom with different subject matter from what you teach).

Step Three: Whenever you observe a school it is important to take good field notes, including detailed records of the date, time, and exact location of your observations, as well as significant numbers (such as how many people were present) and significant demographic data (e.g., of those present, how many were "male" or "special education students"?) You could make a dated observation chart containing the following types of information:

- **Scope and Context of Observation:** Describe exactly what you observed (grade, subject, activity), when (time of day), and for how long the observation took place.
- **Who Was Present:** This could be as simple as one teacher and fifteen students, however, try to get more granular if you can. For example: Was the class was made up entirely of students of color? Was there a larger ratio of girls to boys? Were some of the students bilingual or ELLs?
- **Ease of Access:** Did you have to get permissions? If so, from whom? To what extent was there "buy-in" from key participants and gatekeepers such as administrators, teachers and students?
- **Your Role:** To what extent were you a participant observer? How did you introduce yourself, or were you introduced to the group at all? Where did you situate yourself, and were you free to move around and talk? Did you have the power to intervene, such as stopping the action to ask a clarifying question, or consciously change directions? Did you have a pre-existing relationship with all or any of the participants? Did you share a critical characteristic of the group members such as common race, ethnicity, gender, or language?
- **Activities and Interactions:** What are you seeing in practice? First, consider that what you see may be viewed from both a *wide angle* and *narrow-angle* lens. This means that sometimes you may sit-in on a small group activity, while other times you may be observing the entire class. Second, you will be looking to see factors such as: how are students seated, and who decides this? How much movement is there? Who is at the "center" of the room (if anyone)?
- **Voice and Conversation:** On a basic level this is looking at who talks, to whom, and what they have to say. But there are much more complex issues here to consider that have to do with agency and power (see below).
- **Agency and Power:** What are the explicit and implicit rules for talking in the classroom? Who listens? Who is allowed to redirect or "silence" the conversation? Who makes what significant decisions? Who has the power to object?
- **Nonverbal Factors:** For example, are some students doodling in their notebooks, nonverbally communicating with other students, eye-rolling, or texting? Does the teacher use hand-signals or facial expressions to direct, reward or punish students?
- **Subtle Factors:** This could include a range of things that might not be immediately obvious but that could become clear under more focused observation, such as whether it is particularly cold in the classroom, whether a lot of students are absent that day, whether the teacher is going through material too quickly for the students to keep up.

Critical Questions

- How did you decide what to pay most attention to, especially when there were competing options or factors?
- What struck you (or surprised you) the most? Why did this stand out?
- With what did you connect most personally? Why did this resonate for you?
- What perplexed you the most? What about it didn't you understand? How could you find out answers to your questions?
- What assumptions were challenged for you? Why and how?
- "If the shared culture of the school I visited was a *living thing*, what would it look, feel, and act like? If that living thing could talk, what would it say to us? If it could develop, what would it morph into next? What aspects of the culture (good and bad) allow it to thrive? What aspects (good and bad) are hindering its further development?" (Credit: Sam Chaltain, p. 49)
- If you did this assignment as part of a "pair" how did your observations and answers to the stated questions differ from those of your partner? Can you think of any reason why you might have had different experiences looking at the same thing?

QUESTIONS FOR CLASSROOM DISCUSSION

- Based on what you already "knew" or thought you knew about the schools being observed, were you surprised by your classmates' observations and answers to the stated questions?
- What themes and disjunctions did you find among your classmates' observations? In what ways were these reflective of the school itself?
- If you observed the same school, compare your observations to your classmates.

TRANSGRESSIVE VOICES

The following three excerpts from candidates' weekly journals are reflective of how observing schools as "living entities" allows practitioners to see contradictions as well as continuities in practice. The first excerpt is an example of the disjunction between what teachers perceive to be their priorities versus what administrators pay attention to when observing the classroom. Elyse is perplexed by the fact that after observing her classroom an administrator ignored everything but the fact that some students were "chewing gum" essentially ignoring the complex nature of teaching and teacher-student interactions. In the second reflection, Randall observes and laments the "robotic" nature and "prison-like" environment of his classroom and school, wherein students follow strict daily procedures and routines which he feels robs the classroom of creativity and diversity and causes students to "act out as a form of resistance." By contrast, the last example is a positive reflection on what happened when a school principal had teachers go on a "community walk" as a way of helping teachers "become aware of the other needs and characteristics that each child has that I had not learned by sitting in the classroom with them" and ultimately create a more culturally relevant experience for them in the classroom. According to Thomas: "The community walk was not only beneficial for me to understand my students, but it also helped me to plan meaningful lessons that relate to their lives outside of school."

Elyse

One specific event that caused a shift in my attention was when an administrator came into my class during first period, at which point I had my most challenging group of students. This group of students is my "lowest cohort," the term that our staff uses informally to describe the cohort that has the lowest average math and reading scores. Unsurprisingly, this group has the most behavior issues and requires my best efforts at classroom management at all times. That morning, I had them all sitting down and about eighty percent of them were on task in the first five minutes. This is a higher statistic than usual, so I was feeling pleased as my administrator was observing. Then, she came up to me and commented that, "four students have gum in their mouths, and I need you to do something about it." Her comment surprised me, because it was not the feedback I was expecting, considering the kind of behavior issues that our team has had with this group. I felt that having a majority on task, quiet, and relatively focused was something to be commended. So, hearing this feedback discouraged me in the moment, and seemed to sweep the rug out from underneath me as I started class with them.

Additionally, it was feedback focused on something that seemed to be so arbitrary. Will gum-chewing help or hinder their learning? Later that day, the same administrator came to my room to follow up. She said that after she gave me the feedback about the gum, she looked back into the room and saw that students were still chewing gum. She then asked me what my protocol was for this, as gum is strictly prohibited. I replied to her honestly, saying that it wasn't my top priority with that particular group of students. There are so many other things I have to think about in the moment at the beginning of class that gum-chewing falls to the end of the list. I admitted that this may not be the ideal way to handle things as their teacher, but it was the truth. She seemed to appreciate my honesty but continued to ask how she could support me. Really, I thought, she could support me by understanding the amount of things I had to consider in the first five minutes of a class period, and to understand that addressing gum-chewing was not the feedback I needed in the moment. In the first five minutes, there is a lot going on:

- Make sure ppt is at the right spot for the class when they enter, but be at your door between bells.
- Hand out worksheet for the day as students enter.
- Greet each student by name.
- Start the Do Now timer.
- Observe the room to make sure students are in their assigned seats.
- Take paper attendance to track absent/late students.
- Check uniforms and give demerits.
- Check for contraband and give demerits.
- Check that all students are in their assigned seats.
- Manage behavior—students not sitting down, talking, cursing.
- Follow behavior cycle for these—warning, demerit, demerit.
- Make sure students are getting their notebooks out and getting started.
- Check homework and track it on clipboard.
- Late students enter: check their pass for the time, or give a late demerit and then get them settled while maintaining what you have already started with the rest of class.
- Answer questions from the students.

After writing everything down, I felt validated by the fact that there was indeed a lot going on. I wanted to show this to my administrator and say, "THIS is why students were chewing gum in my class. There is too much to think about, and gum is not a priority." When someone gives feedback that seems to undercut all of those efforts, it damages the teacher-administrator relationship.

Randall

I believe as a person of color that I am extremely frustrated because I see the reality for the community I serve, and I know the students can rise above their circumstances with proper support. I feel like I take student failure more personally than most of my co-workers and it is hard to challenge the inferiority accepted by the adults and students. The robotic nature of the classroom structure and the way that I have been delivering the content is not creating an exciting learning environment. The do-now, modeling, independent practice and exit ticket format expected to be used this year in instruction has taken some of the diversity out of the classroom. I feel strongly that the poverty my students experience allows for them to be robbed of a thriving educational experience.

In addition, the lack of investment in students is obvious and because these students learn at a young age that they go to an underperforming school that lacks a host of resources from appropriate desks to books. The low expectation for our kids allows them to often be ignored and the lack of resources to virtually go unaddressed. The system itself is set up to keep poor people of color disempowered and just content with surviving. In addition, the school to prison pipeline is well known yet the schools continue to operate in a way that appeases white America and disenfranchises students of color. I have come to realize they are acting out as a form of resistance to the oppressive restraints placed on them in school. We even police the times they can go to the bathroom and get up from their seat to stretch or retrieve something from their book bag.

The prison-like function of urban schools is preparing our students to be told what to do and lose their autonomy. As someone who identifies with my students, I realize that I must deliver certain culturally responsive lessons and be brutally honest with the room full of black students who have different obstacles to overcome than their white peers would face. My students do not have the privilege to be ignorant.

Thomas

On Election Day this year my principal started off the morning of our professional development with a community walk. He said that we as teachers, and as one of the most important people in our students' lives, need to understand where our students come from and what their stories are. It was not until I was physically put into the child's environment when I realized that the characteristics and needs of children at certain ages are not the same. This community walk helped me to become aware of the other needs and characteristics that each child has that I had not learned by sitting in the classroom with them. I was able to understand my students by speaking with them in the classroom and discussing their different life events, however, I really got a sense of where my students were from and what their home lives were like just by walking around the community. I reflected on this walk and used my new knowledge of my students to provide culturally responsive lesson plans.

My students typically have a writing prompt related to the story that we read that week. However, this time I wanted to relate the writing prompt to their personal lives. I allowed them to draw pictures and write about their favorite activity to do after school and have them talk about why they love to do this particular activity. I was able to really get a sense of what my students do when they leave the school from this writing experiment. The community walk was not only beneficial for me to understand my students, but it also helped me to plan meaningful lessons that relate to their lives outside of school. By changing my prompt to make it specific to my children, I was able to give them the opportunity to open up and become comfortable with their learning. I also felt more comfortable talking to my students about their home lives.

Chapter Seven

Walking Hip and Lip

*Strategy: (Re)Choreographing
the Anime of Student Movement*

"Within organizational routines, it is in the performative aspect in which biases have their greatest impact. The rules, written with careful neutrality and legitimizing universality, are undermined by the social meaning of race in social interaction. Attending to the daily performance of disciplinary routines is essential to understanding the experiences of students within them and challenging the racial disproportionality that often results. . . . Disciplinary routines are just one arena in which blackness carries a kind of racial penalty that leads to increased surveillance, restricted freedom of movement, and suspicion about one's intentions."—Diamond and Lewis, 2019, pp. 845 and 852

Key Concepts

Performative Organizational Routines, Racialized Movement, Student Autonomy, Surveillance, and Restricted Freedom of Movement

Goals

- To reflect on the ways that schools exert power over students' performative routines and movement both as a means of control and also as a racialized discourse.
- To unpack the motivation behind and impact of robotic discipline policies that serve to militarize students.
- To imagine ways in which teachers and schools might challenge these policies and consider the long-term consequences for low-income students of color.

ABOUT STUDENT MOVEMENT IN SCHOOLS

As Diamond and Lewis (2019, pp. 835–836) note in their study of discipline and school routines at a mixed-race high school: "Schools (and all organizations) partly function through the operation of organizational routines" which include "the collective daily practices that people engage in to get things done." On the surface, these routines are usually crafted to be fair to all students, and race neutral, however that is not always how they are practiced or perceived. According to Diamond and Lewis (p. 837), "This is because of the way race works symbolically (the meaning and values people attach to members of different racial groups) and structurally (affecting who has access to certain kinds of resources), when real people interact in specific contexts."

The idea that students should be "silent" and "orderly" when they walk in school hallways is not a particularly controversial one. The rationale is obvious: Students should not disturb other classrooms in practice. Students shouldn't have the opportunity to damage or vandalize school property. Students must be restrained from the urge to get into verbal or physical altercations with other students, thus threatening everyone's safety and serenity. Students need to stay focused as they transition from one activity or subject to the next. Students need to practice and learn "self-control" at an early age.

While all schools have expectations and rules about how children should conduct themselves in public spaces, urban schools with high percentages of students of color tend to craft and enforce these rules to an extreme. Sometimes the justification is that urban teachers typically have much larger student bodies to take care of (or keep track of depending on how you look at it), that it is important in overcrowded schools to keep students of different age groups from clashing, or that many urban schools are housed in older buildings with areas that are structurally unsafe to walk through. Fair enough.

The fact that urban schools are overwhelmingly filled with poor students, students of color, immigrants, English Language Learners, and students deemed "special education," however, is not irrelevant here. Having expectations for order and safety in school hallways is not controversial, but the ways in which we teach students these values and skills is. Many more affluent schools teach it (or model it) under the rubrics of respect, engagement, and comaraderie. Students are encouraged to move and act in certain ways as a sign of dignity and self-respect and of being part of a larger community. Less affluent schools, by contrast, model and practice policies of surveillance, intimidation, shaming, and punishment.

Rules such as "Hip and Lip," for example, regulate students' movement and behavior in almost militaristic or robotic ways, relying on the assumption that this is the only way that certain students can be sufficiently "managed" (i.e., controlled, tamed, restrained, pacified). The underlying (and often unspoken) assumption about how children can "move" in public spaces is deeply entwined in issues of race, class and gender—quite similar actually to the underlying assumptions about poor Black males in public spaces. Recent news stories of the tragic deaths of Black men who appear to be "threatening," for example, have led to the #Blacklivesmatter movement, and to a national outpouring of dissent and despair that minorities—male, female or non-binary—are still treated with suspicion and undue violence primarily due to the color of their skin.

Research on school discipline policies have emphasized that for poor students and students of color—particularly Black and Latino boys—fear is at the center of teacher-student interactions and relationships. According to Gregory et al. (2010, p. 63), "Given stereotypes and media portrayals of Black youth as dangerous and aggressive . . . teacher expectations for behavior may also influence whether these students are selected for discipline sanctions." This then becomes a vicious cycle as the more that Black students are singled out for disciplinary sanctions while in school, the more engrained the stereotype of Black youth being dangerous or aggressive in general becomes. As Goodman (2013, p. 94) notes in her study of Charter Management Operated (CMO) schools which tend to have much stricter discipline policies, many low-income students and students of color have begun to internalize messages of constraint. When asked how they felt about such restrictive policies, one student responded, for example, that "Unconstrained moments were opportunities for 'bad choices' or 'wasting time.'" According to Goodman: "For most of these students, freedom is associated with an untamed spirit. Those possessing it are likely to do bad things and get into trouble" (p. 94).

Examples 1–3 come from practicing teachers, who describe how they teach students "self-regulation." What these policies have in common is the idea that the teacher is the only authority or leader that can regulate movement, and that students must comply flawlessly with the teacher's commands—even when they make no sense. The message of "override" is one that reinforcing the idea that those who are less powerful (e.g., minorities) must not be allowed to trust their own instincts or get too comfortable with their environment and sense of logic. Instead of students feeling empowered and acting on individual agency, students must always be willing to "play" according to the conductor's command. They must always be willing to "mimic" those in control. Even worse, they are pitted against one another so that even among those less powerful someone must be a "loser." Perhaps most disturbingly, the idea is to get students "accustomed to the game," a not very subtle way of admitting that self-regulation is less about individual dignity than about knowing one's place.

Example #1: Conducting an Orchestra

This activity requires the use of musical instruments. The teacher will have a long stick or ruler and will act like an orchestra leader, conducting when they will play their instruments. The teacher will wave the conductor's wand quickly or slowly and have students play according to the teacher's movements. Then, the teacher will have students override their automatic response by indicating that students should play slowly when she waves the conductors wand quickly, and vice versa.

Example #2: Head-Shoulders-Knees-Toes

This activity requires that students override an automatic response, and therefore exhibit self-regulation. Begin by having students point to their head, shoulders, knees and toes. Have students touch each body part in a variety of sequences to get accustomed to the game. Then have students override their automatic response by asking students to point to incongruent body parts. For example, tell students "When I say to touch your head, touch your TOES!!" or "When I say touch your tummy, touch your EARS."

Example #3: Stance Contest

Two students stand and face each other in a specific pose (any pose that they choose). When the teacher says "GO," neither student may move, talk, or change facial expression. The first student to do so loses. The teacher can also come up with the poses if she wants so that they have someone to mimic.

Examples 4 and 5 show some strategies, also shared by practicing teachers on-line, specifically designed to regulate students when they walk down the hallways.

Example #4: Line Up Call & Response

"I do this with my kinders every time we line up to go somewhere (and enforce it in the entire way until we get where we're going). Say it like a military drill sergeant:

> Teacher: Facing?
> Students: Forward!
> T: Arms?
> S: Crossed!
> T: Mouths (or lips)?
> S: Quiet! (or zipped!)
> T: Bodies?

S: Still!

then I can remind the kids what they said before we left (you told me your arms were crossed so you need to keep them that way). It works like a charm for me!"

Example #5: Line Poem

> Every time I walk in line
> I stand so straight and tall
> I keep my arms down by my side
> they do not move at all
> My head is facing forward
> My eyes look straight ahead
> My lips are closed
> I am listening to what is said.
> No one will hear me
> I will be so quiet
> That's how I walk in line!
> —http://www.proteacher.net/discussions/showthread.php?t=14827

What these strategies have in common is painfully obvious: Students as young as kindergarten are treated as if they are in the military, expected to speak in unison, on command, and to essentially give up their right to any form of free movement, expression, and speech. It may sound extreme, but we are teaching them to disassociate from their bodies by keeping them "still" and to silence their voices by "zipping" their lips. And just to make the point even more strongly, we ask them to repeat poems with lines such as: "No one will hear me." That we ask poor and students of color to say this out loud in the form of an "affirmation" is not just ironic, it is demoralizing, racist, and oppressive.

In example 6—titled Spies—it may seem on first glance that the teacher is trying to find a way to make obedience "fun" and kid-friendly but look closely. One must raise the question: What kind of stress are we putting on small children when every time they walk down the hall they have to imagine being eaten by Alligators? What are the short- and long-term impacts of having students collectively do a "Whew" (wipe their hand across our fore-head) when they reach their destination? This does not seem like a good practice for any young child, but it can be especially stressful for students who live in neighborhoods with high crime and violence rates. It is not a "game" for them. Tiptoeing past doorways and ducking under windows may well be a survival strategy. Reinforcing this anxiety in schools, which are supposed to be safe and nurturing environments, seems a highly dubious idea.

Example #6: Spies

I teach 1st grade and I like to mix it up. At the beginning of the year we are "Spies." We try to go down the hall so quietly no one even looks at us. We tip toe past doorways and duck under windows. We all do a "Whew" (wipe our hand across our forehead) when we reach our destination. Sometimes we are frogs, and if we are quiet we won't get eaten by Alligators. Sometimes we have to catch a bubble in our mouth and hold it (hold air in checks like a bubble).

STRATEGY

Step One: Consider some of the discipline policies and practices you grew up with in school regarding movement and speech—especially in public spaces like school hallways. In what ways, if at all, was your movement regulated? What body stances (if any) were you required to pose? What kinds of chants and rhymes did you have to recite? What were the consequences for not following the rules? How did you *feel* when walking in public spaces in school? If these movements were "dances," what kind of dances would they be? Ballet, jazz, tap, hip hop? Were there different "dances" for different areas of the school? Were other students doing the same "dance" you were? *Can you find a candid photograph of yourself in school, or draw a picture of how you remember your body in school?*

Step Two: Consider the same questions above, but now about the policies and practices regarding movement and speech at the school you currently teach (or student teach) at. What are the stated rationales (if any) of these policies and practices? How are they explained to teachers? How are they explained to students? Are different groups of students subject to different rules? Again, consider how you would choreograph these movements. *Can you take a photograph or draw a picture of how your school expects students to pose and interact?*

Step Three: If possible, put the two photos side by side and compare them.

CRITICAL REFLECTION QUESTIONS

- What do the dances you grew up doing look like when contrasted to those you now direct? What does your present school picture look like in contrast to your own images/memories of school?
- What do you believe are the hidden assumptions and messages inherent in these practices? What direct or subtle messages do you think children

receive when they engage these policies? What is at stake for those students who practice dissent?

- How do these ideologies reflect larger societal beliefs about race, class, gender, and sexual identity?
- If possible, ask your students how these policies make them *feel* (for younger children, you can ask them to draw or act out their feelings instead of or in addition to writing prompts).
- In light of these questions and feedback from students, (how) would you change these policies and practices, or *re-choreograph* the dance?
- What would be the possible results of these changes—both positive and negative?

QUESTIONS FOR CLASSROOM DISCUSSION

Compare you own personal experience with movement in the school you attended or observed with those of other candidates in your class.

- In what ways were they the same or different?
- Do you see any patterns between the policies and the demographics of the schools?

TRANSGRESSIVE VOICES

The following excerpts from candidates' weekly journals illustrate the confusion and frustration that many students feel when the school has strict restrictions as to how they can move their bodies. In the first excerpt Leah describes a list of rules that all students change every morning after reciting the Pledge of Allegiance. While ostensibly about issues of caring and kindness, the recitation includes lines such as: "Hands are for helping" and "Always raise your hand." As Leah observes: "These codes manifest in our students' understanding of the world around them" and further suggests that students interpret these rules so literally that they are ultimately confused when the rules are taken out of context (such as when they read a story about a dinosaur who went to school and accidently broke something with his hands rather than using them for "helping"). Leah also suggests that the recitation is way too prescribed, noting that feet may be for walking, but they are also for dancing.

In the second excerpt, Enrique reflects on his school's policy where kindergarten students must walk down the hallways and other common spaces "Hip and Lip," which literally means one hand on their hip and one hand on their lips. Enrique inquires: "How are we supposed to encourage students to become active thinkers when we are silencing them to the point of them covering their lips with their fingers?" and further notes that students in schools in wealthier White districts have significantly more freedom. After directly asking students how they feel about walking hip and lip, he finds that they not only dislike it, but that it literally "hurts their arms hands" and symbolically it makes them feel less human.

Leah

My school utilizes school wide behavior statements. Each morning after the Pledge of Allegiance, all students recite the school rules:

> Hands are for helping, hands are for helping.
> Eyes are for watching, eyes are for watching.
> Ears are for listening, ears are for listening.
> Mouths are for kind words, mouths are for kind words.
> Feet are for walking, feet are for walking,
> Hearts are for caring, hearts are for caring.
> Always raise your hand, always raise your hand.

These school rules grace the wall of my first grade classroom, an anchor chart that we chant following the pledge of allegiance each day. These codes manifest in our students' understanding of the world around them. One day while reading "When Dinosaurs Go to School," a student exclaimed that the dinosaur was not using his hands to help when the dinosaur broke something in the classroom. While I was pleased that my students had internalized using their hands to help, I was wary. Did these school rules address the issues that get students in trouble? What are our expectations for little kids? Ultimately, I have found that these school rules provide a foundation but leave out many of the wonderful things that we can accomplish in school. Hands are not just for helping; they also give high fives. Sometimes feet aren't for walking; they are for dancing. While I appreciate the starting point, my students need more flexibility as they come to understand the world and what school expects of them.

Enrique

Hip and lip is the position students are expected to walk in whenever they are moving about the school in the hallways or other common spaces. This position forces students to walk with one hand on their hip, and the other holding their finger over their lip. The hand on the hip is to keep students from touching anything or fooling around with their friends. The finger over the lip signifies the voiceless way in which the student is expected to walk. How are we supposed to encourage students to become active thinkers when we are silencing them to the point of them covering their lips with their fingers? It is interesting that society feels that students from a very specific background are the ones who need these strict discipline policies. Why do kindergarten students of color in Camden, NJ need to walk down the hallways silent with one hand over their lip and the other on their hip, when students in wealthy suburban schools are able to walk freely? My students were then asked how they feel when they are asked to walk hip and lip in the hallways. Some of the comments regarding hip and lip are as follows:

- "I don't like it because when you do this (shows hip and lip) sometimes it feels like I am going in the trash can and eating it. It makes me feel so bad like that."
- "I don't like it because it hurts my arms."
- "When I walk other places I just feel right because I can do what I like."
- "I hate it because my hands hurt."
- "I think it's dumb, I don't like it, I hate it, because every time I do it I can't keep doing it."

The act of walking hip and lip in the hallways is stripping students of simple freedoms that they deserve. It is almost prison-like that they are forced to cover their lips and put their hands on their hips while walking through common spaces. A five-year-old student has a hard time sitting still for seconds at a time, and walking hip and lip in the hallway can be extremely difficult for them. It is frightening that some students feel as if they have to break this rule outside of school in order to feel better.

Chapter Eight

Thinking Like a Policymaker

Strategy: Design Thinking

"We must resist the urge to solve new problems with old thinking, we must be aware of the symptomatic solution. . . . Keep asking, 'What behaviors are we rewarding?'"—Chaltain, 2009, pp. 42 and 81

Key Concepts

Design Thinking and Policymaking

Goals

- Understand the ways that policymakers define educational problems, assert the need for reform, and test the impact of different interventions and strategies.
- Use metaphors to reflect on and critically assess the ways that differences in student achievement are framed.
- Consider the ways in which educational reforms are often driven by competing or converging interests that can reflect "struggles over values, worldviews, and underlying ideologies."
- Analyze the ways in which the same educational reform can impact different stakeholder groups in different ways, foregrounding the need to ask the question: Who benefits?

ABOUT DESIGN THINKING AND POLICYMAKING

Design Thinking is an iterative and cyclical process used to challenge assumptions, reframe the definition and source of problems, and create alternative strategies and solutions. While many people associate it with product and service design—for example, design thinking was used in developing Uber Eats—it is also used in policymaking and can be a critical tool in designing and evaluating school reform policies. At the heart of design thinking is the idea that in order to truly understand what you are "designing," you need to emphasize with the people who will ultimately be impacted by your design. Another key feature of design thinking is looking at problems from a systemic viewpoint. In other words, it is important to understand the roots of the problem. Finally, design thinking emphasizes "out of the box" solutions. As Chaltain (2009, p. 91) reminds us, "We must resist the urge to solve new problems with old thinking," and "allowing yourself to be uncertain of what will emerge is the threshold we must pass though for new ways of being to take root."

Sometimes these solutions are elusive because we become accustomed to looking at things in the same way and close off our mind to different perspectives. One way of breaking this pattern is to solve a problem in one context and then apply these same solutions to another context. For example, how we deal with a playground that is unsafe for kids to play on due to structural imperfections might provide insight into how we redesign school curricula to better engage students. They seem like, and are, very different problems, however, when looking for root causes one might find similarities. From the perspective of children, they want the same outcome: To interact in an environment that is safe, fun, engaging, and ultimately a positive experience. The activity in this chapter guides candidates through the design thinking process by comparing and attempting to solve what seem like two very different problems. After brainstorming solutions to the first problem, candidates are asked to consider what would happen if they applied similar solutions to the second problem. A key component of this strategy addressed throughout this process is thinking about who benefits from particular solutions, and what is the likely impact on different stakeholder groups.

STRATEGY

Step One: Pretend that you are a member of a town counsel and you have been asked to solve the following problem. There is a steep hill with lots of trees and boulders in the middle of a town, and children are always falling down the hill and hurting themselves. Some children are fine, but others have bruises, some break arms or legs, and some children have head injuries. The hill is currently the only place in town where children can play. What solutions can you think of to this problem? (This particular example was inspired by educator Herbert Kohl.) Write your solutions in the chart on the next page, including considerations that accompany each solution. Then consider where there might be areas of interest convergence, meaning that the solutions that are chosen provide explicit or implicit benefits for key stakeholders. *Examples are included to get you started.*

Step Two: Pretend that you are a member of a school board and you have been asked to solve the following problem. There is a wide academic "achievement gap" among students in your school district. Some students do very well in school-based or standardized tests while other students are not "proficient" or meeting "adequate yearly progress" measures. Certain groups of children are considered to be especially "at-risk." These children are falling behind and missing out on important opportunities. In addition, some schools in the district score much more highly than others. What solutions can you think of to "close" the "achievement gap"? *As you fill in the chart consider the strategies you used in the previous problem with "the hill." Do any of them transfer over?*

CRITICAL DISCUSSION QUESTIONS

- Did using the metaphorical strategy about the hill enable you to think more creatively (outside the box) about the problems of educational equity and student achievement? In what ways?
- What broad-based "strategies" did you carry over from the first problem to the second?
- How did your "considerations" change when you used the same basic strategy in a completely different context?
- Can you go back through your considerations and match them to different stakeholder groups? How would these problems and solutions look differently from the perspective of teachers, families, children, funders, taxpayers, public services, private companies, etc.?
- After doing this exercise, how has your understanding of the "student achievement gap" and other educational policies expanded or changed?

QUESTIONS FOR CLASSROOM DISCUSSION

- How did your problem-solving strategies line up with or differ from those of your classmates in regard to both the first and second problems?
- Did you have similar "considerations" for each strategy? If not, were you surprised by some of the considerations your classmates thought of?

Table 8.1. Strategy: Design Thinking

Solution	Considerations	Who Benefits?
Example: Hire a professional company to come and chop down all of the trees and remove the boulders on the hill. The company would come back for upkeep as needed.	Where would the money come from to pay for this? The current district or city budget? Additional taxes? Charitable contributions? Government grants? Who would decide what company gets the contract and on what criteria? What if the company does a poor job of maintenance and children are still getting hurt?	
Example: Only let the most athletic or careful children play on the hill. Ban other clumsy or "at-risk" children from playing there.	How would you know which children are the most athletic or careful? What kinds of pre-tests would you need to do before deciding? Who would administer the tests and how often would children need to be retested? What would the children who are banned from the hill do instead?	
Example: Build a hospital at the bottom of the hill to take care of children's injuries.	Will it be "too late" for children whose injuries are severe? What about families that don't have health insurance? How will the hospital prioritize who gets attention first—will it be first come first serve or based on the severity of injuries?	
Example: Redirect children to play in another town where the hills are safer.	What about children who live too far or don't have transportation to get to the new town? What if the other town doesn't want "outsider" children on their hills? What if the other town's hills get too crowded or start deteriorating from too much use?	

- After discussing your strategies with the rest of your classmates, how has your understanding of the "student achievement gap" expanded or changed?

TRANSGRESSIVE VOICES

The following excerpts from candidates' weekly journals reflect the conflicts associated in educational contexts that prioritize high stakes testing. In the first excerpt Malachi expresses his frustration with his school's expectations that students will be able to achieve a 52% increase in biology proficiency in just three and a half months. What bothers Malachi the most is that fact: "Proposed solutions to problems are often met with the phrase, 'well we can't do that because we've never done that before,' and I find it extremely frustrating when this mentality is applied to my suggestions to improve student outcomes." This is a particularly salient example of how many policymakers and educational leaders are resistant to thinking "outside the box" and considering approaching the problem in novel ways from different perspectives. In the second excerpt Rita laments that ignoring testing mandates will result in the loss of federal funding and wonders how she can balance "teaching in compliance for a test" with offering "students a better quality of education that may not appear on a test." The pressure to raise test scores conflicts with her belief that "being a teacher is also about learning from students" and that she must be open to "teachable moments" even when she herself is the one learning. Rita's passage illustrates the issues that arise for teachers when they are boxed in by a particular mandate (standardized testing) rather than given the leeway and creativity to address the problem in new ways.

Malachi

While I could write volumes about my negative experiences with the school's administration, I will limit myself to the describing the one thing which affects me the most: the administration's extreme aversion to taking suggestions from teachers and trying to apply new solutions to identified problems. Proposed solutions to problems are often met with the phrase, "well we can't do that because we've never done that before," and I find it extremely frustrating when this mentality is applied to my suggestions to improve student outcomes. For example, last year approximately 28% of students passed the Biology Keystone exam, and the school has set a goal for 80% of students to be proficient this year. That is a huge amount of growth for one year. I am a staunch believer that if you want to see a radical change you need a radical solution. Because the school runs on a block schedule, the entire Biology curriculum must be taught in a single semester, which is a huge amount of content to cover in 3½ months. It is important to note that Math and English (the other subjects with Keystone exams) are taught for a full school year before students are tested. In a curriculum meeting earlier this year, I presented three different ways that students could receive a full year of Biology instruction before being tested, and each was shot down because it had never been done before. It is so frustrating to be trapped in a static school environment without a voice, and even more frustrating to know that this paralyzing stasis is caused by poor decisions made by a weak administration.

Jonah

At first in the journaling process, I found myself honed in on the flaws with my students' behavior. I became focused on what students were doing wrong, and specifically each student's behavioral challenges. As the journaling process continued, I found myself more concentrated on what I was saying or doing to my students when this was occurring. Focusing on the way I spoke to my students goes hand in hand with what I noticed next: I began to realize that speaking to them effectively is incredibly different than simply "dealing with" the problem. Many times, I found myself saying, "no," easily to a child in my classroom, or "please just finish your work." This is dealing with a problem, and not attempting to find a solution to the problem. Dealing with the problem does not positively affect my students in any way. I found that I began to focus more on how to solve the problem by figuring out what my children need in order to work, and how I could be speaking to them to benefit them. My understandings of my students' as learners has prominently changed.

One of the largest understandings I have come to learn and understand is that students act a certain way for a reason. If they are disinterested in a topic, off task, or simply refuse to do their work, there is almost always a reason behind it, whether it has to do with their academic level, something with friends, teachers, or even at home. Having this understanding of my students has drastically helped me be able to better guide them and assist them in the work that we do in our classroom every day. I have come to learn that my students enjoy learning new things constantly and giving them new materials to work with helps them learn, but also allows them to take ownership over their work. When they learn something new on their own, that is when I see my students light up, and truly take pride in their work.

Rita

The issues I have focused on all seem to point in the direction of the problematic high stakes testing. It is because of high stakes testing, that administrators and teachers have a difficult time cultivating the whole student. Could we really afford casting the testing concerns to the side and address the cultivation of a students' complete self with the fear of losing federal funding (even if it is minute in some instances)? From my understanding, high stakes testing does not provide most schools with many advantages anyway. Rather they are trapped in an endless cycle of performing low, receiving less funds, receiving mediocre instruction and leadership, then the cycle repeats. To make matters worse, policies are in place that force administrators and teachers to adhere to a test-taking way of teaching and leading school, meanwhile forfeiting opportunities for students to gain higher-order thinking skills. But how can we as teachers balance the two: teaching in compliance for a test and offer students a better quality of education that may not appear on a test?

Now I am equipped with the understanding that being a teacher is not just about learning information, teaching it, then monitoring success based on how well students can regurgitate the information back verbatim. Being a teacher is also about learning from students, challenging norms, being creative and learning from all experiences and walks of life because they all have value. In order to encourage the cultivation of a student's life, holistically, I must continue to encourage students to take actions towards the principles they believe in. Students should want to share their experiences and journeys because each story is unique and distinctive to them. But in order to create a safe environment for this level of expression, I must also be willing to listen with my ears and heart when students are communicating what is of value to them. I must be open to teachable moments, even when I am being taught.

Conclusion

A Call to Action

As noted in the preface, the activities and strategies in this book came out of my own work as a teacher educator and my own deep commitment to helping my candidates think more critically about what it means to be a teacher in an education system founded on and fueled by systemic inequities. As I finish writing this book, I find that I am acutely aware that many of the transgressive voices included present an extremely negative picture of urban education, teaching in public education, and the educational experiences, opportunities, and expectations for low-income students of color and other marginalized students. It was not my intent to further add to the discourses of "hopelessness" or even of "blame." My intent is not to dissuade candidates from becoming teachers or to suggest that after engaging with this book they will now be fully prepared to face what lies in front of them. There is no doubt that, at some point, nearly every teacher will feel "forced to facilitate policies that they do not agree with" and will feel "silenced." As teacher educators, however, there is much that we can do to help our candidates be successful change agents and advocates of social justice in their schools, but we do need to make some significant changes in the way we prepare them.

I think it is critical that we listen carefully to these transgressive voices—voices of real teacher candidates who are committed to furthering educational equity, diversity and inclusion—because we cannot afford to lose them. Our schools need them. Our students need them. Our candidates struggle with their belief that they can be transformational and their fears that this work is "not sustainable," as one former candidate wrote in her journal:

> Why is teaching in an urban, low-income school so difficult? Does teaching
> have to be this hard? Why is it that one of the most important jobs in our
> society is also the one that seems to be the most scarcely resourced? When do
> teachers feel the most successful in their roles in urban, low-income schools?
> What do teachers need in order to feel successful in their roles in urban, low-
> income schools? What kinds of supports are most helpful to teachers? What
> would make teaching easier? If teachers could change one thing about their
> jobs, what would it be? What are the most important factors teachers consider
> when choosing a school at which to teach? I have never been challenged like
> this. This is challenging on a physical, emotional, social, mental level to the
> extreme. It challenges every part of my being.

Although this same candidate went on to add that the very reasons why
teaching challenges her are among the reasons why she loves it, mainly that
"It requires me to use my entire self," she fears that relying on the "work and
dedication of people who are willing to sacrifice themselves to this level"
will lead potentially transformative teachers to leave the profession, asking:
"Is that sustainable though? Is that fair? Is that the way it should be? When
do people decide that this is too hard? Why do people leave? When will I
leave?

If we continue to promote theories of social justice in our teacher education programs without adequately providing candidates with concrete strategies to be effective advocates for their future students, we will end up doing
exactly what Ashley feared the most: promoting the status quo. Right now,
the status quo is alarming. With exceptionally high dropout rates, we are in
danger of losing students who could be our feature leaders and global problem solvers. As one of my former candidates, Rodney, wrote in his journal,
students have a "habit of quitting before they can fail":

> Students' need is to be heard, know they are cared for and about, and believe
> others think that they can be successful. They need to know that we as teachers
> care not only about grades, but about who they are as people. Education is not
> simply the ability to regurgitate information, it is about being able to overcome
> challenges and many of our students are failing to do so. They fail to show up,
> fail to follow rules, fail to work their hardest because they are not invested and
> do not believe anyone thinks they can succeed. They are adopting a habit of
> quitting before they can fail, like people expect them to.

Teachers must relay to their students that they believe in them and will fight
for them, just as teacher educators need to demonstrate this for their candidates. In conclusion, *transgressing teacher education* depends upon some of
the following Calls to Action for teacher educators:

- Instead of "adding" a culturally diverse text, example, or assignment to your syllabus, consider how you can incorporate issues of equity, diversity and systemic racism *across the curriculum.*
- Don't make "White" the norm and people of color "othered" unless it is to underscore the dangers of and seek to dismantle systemic racial hierarchies.
- Provide candidates with tools such as Critical Discourse Analysis and Design Thinking, which they can apply more broadly to think about educational policy and ideologies from different perspectives and across different stakeholder groups.
- Pay close attention to issues of intersectionality. In doing so be careful not to reify identity categories and to pay close attention to issues of positionality and representation.
- Instead of the standard "educational autobiography" or "teaching philosophy statement" think about ways that candidates can express their identity across different mediums (visual, written, and auditory) and bring in diverse examples of community cultural wealth such as recipes, songs, stories, photographs, quotes, drawings, videos, fabrics, etc.
- As much as possible have your candidates spend critically reflective time in authentic school settings. If they are not already working in these school settings, candidates need to be aware of what it means to be a "participant observer." If they already work in these schools, candidates need to understand the politics of critically assessing their own colleagues and supervisors.
- Reject static notions of teacher training that suggest best practices can be decontextualized. Recognize that schools are "living entities" that are constantly evolving, and that school visions and mission statements need to live in practice.
- Help candidates deconstruct the ways that student "smartness" and "movement" are often embedded in issues of compliance, which are in turn embedded in racialized discourses about privilege and power.
- Encourage your candidates to keep journals and to use these journals to tell counterstories and transgressive narratives.

I would like to conclude this book with a poem, written by one my former candidates, that I think epitomizes the journey, joys and conflicts that come with being a humanistic, caring, reflective, and justice-orientated teacher.

Epilogue

I Wonder
I wonder if my students know
That I dream of them at night.
That they live in my anxieties and consume my fears.
That they monopolize my thoughts and
That they hid behind my tears.
I wonder if my students know
That I wear their hearts on my sleeve.
That they color my memories and send chills down my skin.
That they add melody to my laugh and
That they put a twinkle in my grin.
I wonder if my students know
That I reach far and wide for them.
That they stretch my thinning patience and fan my inner fire.
That they push *all* of my buttons and
That they propel my desire.
I wonder if my students know
That I wish for them on stars.
That they occupy my whispered prayers and make my heart whole.
That they breathe life into my words and
That they recharge my weary soul.
I wonder if my students know
That they are everything I see.
And I wonder if my students think
At least half as highly of me.
—Nicole Alliegro

References

Achinstein, Betty, Rodney Owaga, and Dena Sexton. 2010. "Retaining Teachers of Color: A Pressing Problem and Potential Strategy for 'Hard to Staff' Schools." *Review of Educational Research,* 80, no. 1: 71–107.

Amos, Yukari Takimoto. 2010. "'They Don't Want to Get It!' Interaction Between Minority and White Pre-Service Teachers in a Multicultural Education Class." *Multicultural Education*, 17, no. 4: 31–37.

Apple, Michael. 1996. *Cultural Politics and Education.* Teachers College Press.

Apple, Michael. 2012. *Knowledge, Power and Education.* Routledge.

Apple, Michael. 2014. *Official Knowledge.* Routledge.

Banks, James. 1995. "Multicultural Education and Curriculum Transformation." *Journal of Negro Education*, 64, no. 4: 390–400.

Burciaga, Rebeca, and Rita Kohli. 2018. "Disrupting Whitestream Measures of Quality Teaching: The Community Cultural Wealth of Teachers of Color." *Multicultural Perspectives*, 20 no. 1: 5–12.

Cammarota, Julio. 2011. "From Hopelessness to Hope: Social Justice Pedagogy in Urban Education and Youth Development." *Urban Education*, 46, no. 4: 828–844.

Carey, Roderick. 2014. "A Cultural Analysis of the Achievement Gap Discourse: Challenging the Language and Labels Used in the Work of School Reform." *Urban Education*, 49, no. 4: 440–468.

Carver-Thomas, Desiree. 2018. "Diversifying the Teaching Profession: How to Recruit and Retain Teachers of Color." Learning Policy Institute, 1–44.

Chaltain, Sam. 2009. *American Schools: The Art of Creating a Democratic Learning Community.* Rowman & Littlefield.

Cochran-Smith, Marilyn. 2003. "The Multiple Meanings of Multicultural Teacher Education: A Conceptual Framework." *Teacher Education Quarterly*, 30, no. 2: 7–26.

Crenshaw, Kimberlé, Neil Gotanda, Gary Peller, and Kendall Thomas. 1995. *Critical Race Theory: The Key Writings that Formed the Movement.* New York: The New Press.

Dana, Nancy Fitchman, and Diane Yendol-Hoppey. 2019. *The Reflective Educator's Guide to Classroom Research: Learning to Teach and Teaching to Learn Through Practitioner Inquiry.* Corwin Press.

Darling-Hammond, Linda, and Mildred McLaughlin. 2011. "Policies That Support Professional Development in the Era of Reform." *Phi Delta Kappan*, 92, no. 6: 91–92.

Danielewicz, Jane. 2001. *Teaching Selves: Identity, Pedagogy and Teacher Education.* SUNY Press.

Davis, Lori Patton, and Samuel Museus. 2019. "What Is Deficit Thinking? An Analysis of Conceptualizations of Deficit Thinking and Implications for Scholarly Research." *Currents*, 1, no. 1.

Diamond, John, and Amanda Lewis. 2019. "Race and Discipline at a Racially Mixed High School: Status, Capital, and the Practice of Organizational Routines." *Urban Education*, 54, no. 6: 831–859.

Dilworth, Mary. 1992. *Diversity in Teacher Education: New Expectations.* American Associate of Colleges for Teacher Education.

Duckworth, Angela. 2016. *Grit: The Power of Passion and Perseverance.* Scribner.

Galman, Sally, Cinzia Pica-Smith, and Cynthia Rosenberger. 2010. "Aggressive and Tender Navigations: Teacher Educators Confront Whiteness in Their Practice." *Journal of Teacher Education*, 61, no. 3: 225–236.

Gasman, Marybeth, Andres Castro Samayoa, and Alice Ginsberg. 2016. "A Rich Source for Teachers of Color and Learning: Minority Serving Institutions." Philadelphia, PA: Penn Center for Minority Serving Institutions.

Gibboney, Richard. 1994. *The Stone Trumpet: The Story of Practical School Reform, 1960–1990.* SUNY Press.

Ginsberg, Alice. 1999. *When Policymakers and Practitioners Partner.* Dissertation. University of Pennsylvania.

Ginsberg, Alice. 2012. *Embracing Risk in Urban Education: Curiosity, Creative and Courage in the Era of No Excuses and Relay Race Reform.* Rowman & Littlefield.

Gonzalaz, Norma, Luis Moll, and Cathy Amanti. 2005. *Funds of Knowledge: Theorizing Practices in Households, Communities and Classrooms.* Laurence Earlbaum Associates.

Goodman, Joan. 2013. "Charter Management Organizations and the Regulated Environment: Is It Worth the Price?" *Educational Researcher*, 42, no. 2: 89–96.

Grant, Carl, and Gibson Grant. 2011. "Diversity and Teacher Education" In *Studying Diversity in Teacher Education.* Rowman & Littlefield.

Gregory, Ann, Russell Skiba, and Pedro Noguera. 2010. "The Achievement Gap and the Discipline Gap: Two Sides of the Same Coin?" *Educational Researcher*, 39, no. 1: 59–68.

Gutiérrez, Kris. 2008. "Developing a Sociocritical Literacy in the Third Space." *Reading Research Quarterly*, 43, no. 2: 148–164.

Gutierrez, Rochelle, and Ezekiel Dixon-Roman. 2011. "Beyond Gap Gazing: How Can Thinking about Education Comprehensively Help Us (Re)envision Mathematics?" In *Mapping Equity and Quality in Mathematics Education*, pp. 21–34.

Hambacher, Elyse and Ginn, Katherine. 2021. "Race-Visible Teacher Education: A Review of the Literature from 2002–2018." *Journal of Teacher Education*, 72, no. 3: 329–341.

Hatt, Beth. 2012. "Smartness as Cultural Practice in Schools." *American Educational Research Journal*, 49, no. 3: 438–460.

Herrnstein, Richard, and Murray, Charles. 1994. *The Bell Curve.* The Free Press.

Hess, Frederick. 1998. *Spinning Wheels: The Politics of Urban School Reform.* Brookings Institute Press.

Hollins, Etta. 2011. "Teacher Preparation for Quality Teaching." *Journal of Teacher Education*, 62, no. 4: 395–407.

Hollins, Etta, and M. T. Guzman. 2005. "Research on Preparing Teachers for Diverse Populations." In M. Cochran-Smith & K. M. Zeichner (Eds.), *Studying Teacher Education: The Report of the AERA Panel on Research and Teacher Education* (pp. 477–548). Lawrence Erlbaum Associates Publishers and the American Educational Research Association.

hooks, bell. 1994. *Teaching to Transgress: Education as a Practice of Freedom.* Routledge.

Jackson, Tambra. 2015. "Perspectives and Insights of Preservice Teachers of Color on Developing Culturally Responsive Pedagogy at Predominantly White Institutions." *Action in Teacher Education*, 37, no. 3: 223–237.

Jackson, Tambra, and Rita Kohli. 2016. "Guest Editors Introduction: The State of Teachers of Color." *Equity and Excellence in Education*, 49, no. 1: 1–8.

Katz, Michael, and Mike Rose. 2014. *Public Education Under Siege.* University of Pennsylvania Press.

Kohli, Rita. 2009. "Critical Race Reflections: Valuing the Experiences of Teachers of Color in Teacher Education." *Race Ethnicity and Education*, 12, no. 2: 235–251.

Kohli, Rita. 2018. "Behind Closed Doors: The Impact of Hostile Racial Climates on Urban Teachers of Color." *Urban Education*, 53, no. 3: 307–333.

Kohli, Rita. 2021. *Teachers of Color: Resisting Racism and Reclaiming Education.* Harvard Educational Press.

Kohli, Rita, and Marcus Pizarro. 2016. "Fighting to Educate Our Own: Teachers of Color, Relational Accountability and The Struggle for Racial Justice." *Equity and Excellence in Education*, 49, no. 1: 72–84

Ladson-Billings, Gloria. 2011. "Asking the Right Questions." In *Studying Diversity in Teacher Education.*

Ladson-Billings, Gloria. 2006. "From the Achievement Gap to the Educational Debt: Understanding Achievement in U.S. Schools." *Educational Researcher*, 35, no. 7: 3–12.

Lehman, Chris, and Zac Chase. 2015. *Building School 2.0: How to Create the Schools We Need.* Jossey-Bass.

McIntosh, Peggy. 1989. "White Privilege: Unpacking the Invisible Knapsack." The National SEED Project. Retrieved at: https://nationalseedproject.org/Key-SEED-Texts/white-privilege-unpacking-the-invisible-knapsack

McKinley Jones Brayboy, Brian. 2005. "Toward a Tribal Critical Race Theory in Education." *The Urban Review*, 37, no. 5: 425–445.

Milner, Richard. 2010. "What Does Teacher Education Have to Do with Teaching? Implications for Diversity Studies." *Journal of Teacher Education*, 61, nos. 1–2: 118–131.

Milner, Richard. 2013. "Rethinking Achievement Gap Talk in Urban Education." *Urban Education,* 48, no. 1: 3–8.

Milner, Richard, and Tyrone Howard. 2013. "Counter-narrative as Method: Race, Policy and Research for Teacher Education." *Race, Ethnicity and Education*, 16, no. 4: 536–561.

Montecinos, Carmen. 2004. "Paradoxes in Multicultural Teacher Education: Students of Color Positioned as Objects While Ignored as Subjects." *International Journal of Qualitative Studies in Education*, 27, no. 2: 167–181.

Mullet, Dianna. 2018. "A General Critical Discourse Analysis Framework for Educational Research." *Journal of Advanced Academics,* 29, no. 2: 116–142.

Nelson-Barber, Sharon, and Jean Mitchell. 1992. "Restructuring for Diversity: Five Regional Portraits." In *Diversity in Teacher Education: New Expectations*, edited by Mary Dilworth, 229–265. American Association of Colleges for Teacher Education.

Nieto, Sonia. 2000. "Placing Equity Front and Center: Some Thoughts on Transforming Teacher Education for a New Century." *Journal of Teacher Education*, 51, no. 3: 180–187.

Noguera, Pedro. 2008. *The Trouble with Black Boys . . . and Other Reflections on Race, Equity and the Future of Public Education.* John Wiley and Sons.

Picower, Bree. 2009. "The Unexamined Whiteness of Teaching: How White Teachers Maintain and Enact Dominant Racial Ideologies." *Race, Ethnicity and Education*, 12, no. 2: 197–215.

Pizarro, Marcos, and Rita Kohli. 2020. "'I Stopped Sleeping': Teachers of Color and the Impact of Racial Battle Fatigue." *Urban Education*, 55, no. 7: 967–991.

Pugach, Marleen, Joyce Gomez-Najarro, and Ananya Matewos. 2019. "A Review of Identity in Research on Social Justice in Teacher Education: What Role for Intersectionality?" *Journal of Teacher Education*, 70, no. 3: 206–218.

Quartz, Karen Hunter. 2003. "'Too Angry to Leave': Supporting New Teachers' Commitment to Transform Urban Schools." *Journal of Teacher Education*, 54, no. 2: 99–111.

Rios-Aguilar, Cecila, Judy Marquez Kiyama, Michael Gravitt, and Luis Moll. 2011. "Funds of Knowledge for the Poor and Forms of Capital for the Rich? A Capital Approach to Examining Funds of Knowledge." *Theory and Research in Education,* 9, no. 2: 163–184.

Sleeter, Christine, and Richard Milner. "Researching Successful Efforts in Teacher Education to Diversity Teachers. In *Studying Diversity in Teacher Education.*

Sleeter, Christine, and Jenipher Owuor. 2011. "Research on the Impact of Teacher Preparation to Teach Diverse Students: The Research We Have and the Research We Need." *Action in Teacher Education*, 33, nos. 5–6: 524–536.

Skiba, Russell, and Natasha Williams. 2014. "Are Black Kids Worse? Myths and Facts about Racial Differences in Behavior." The Equity Project at Indiana University. Retrieved at: https://indrc.indiana.edu/tools-resources/pdf-disciplineseries/african_american_differential_behavior_031214.pdf.

Sleeter, Christine. 2016. "Wrestling with Problematics of Whiteness in Teacher Education." *International Journal of Qualitative Studies in Education*, 29, no. 8: 1065–1068.

Sleeter, Christine. 2017. "Critical Race Theory and the Whiteness of Teacher Education." *Urban Education*, 52, no. 2: 155–169.

Solorzano, Daniel G., and Tara J. Yosso. 2001. "Critical Race and LatCrit Theory and Method: Counter-storytelling." *International Journal of Qualitative Studies in Education*, 14, no. 4: 471–495.

Teranishi , Robert. 2002. "Asian Pacific Americans and Critical Race Theory: An Examination of School Racial Climate." *Equity & Excellence in Education*, 35, no. 2: 144–154.

Tolbert, Sara, and Serina Eichelberger. 2014. "Surviving Teacher Education: A Community Capital Framework of Persistence." *Race, Ethnicity and Education*, 19, no. 5: 1–18.

Tyack, David, and Larry Cuban. 1997. *Tinkering Toward Utopia: A Century of Public School Reform*. Harvard University Press.

Uhlenberg, Jeffrey, and Kathleen Brown. 2002. "Racial Gap in Teachers' Perceptions of the Achievement Gap." *Education and Urban Society*, 34, no. 4: 493–530.

Valencia, Richard. 1997. *The Evolution of Deficit Thinking: Educational Thought and Practice*. Falmer Press/Taylor and Francis.

Valencia, Richard. 2010. *Dismantling Deficit Thinking: Education Thought and Practice*. New York: Routledge.

Villegas, Ana Maria, and Jacqueline Jones Irvine. 2010. "Diversifying the Teaching Force: An Examination of Major Arguments." *Urban Review*, 42, no. 3: 175–192.

Yosso, Tara. 2005. "Whose Culture Has Capital? A Critical Race Theory Discussion of Community Cultural Wealth." *Race, Ethnicity and Education*, 8, no. 1: 69–91.

Zeichner, Kenneth. 2006. "Reflections of a University-Based Teacher Educator on the Future of College- and University-Based Teacher Education." *Journal of Teacher Education*, 57, no. 3: 326–340.

Zeichner, Kenneth. 2009. *Teacher Education and the Struggle for Social Justice*. New York: Routledge.

Index

About the Author

Alice E. Ginsberg is a professor of teacher education and higher education, whose research and writing has focused on issues of educational equity, opportunity and inclusion, culturally relevant pedagogy, diversifying the teaching profession, university-school-community partnerships, inquiry- and project-based learning, authentic assessment, educational philanthropy, and urban school reform. She is the author or editor of seven books, including *Embracing Risk in Urban School Reform* (Rowman & Littlefield, 2012), *The Evolution of American Women's Studies* (Palgrave, 2009), and *Gender in Urban Education* (Heinemann, 2004).

Made in United States
North Haven, CT
04 May 2022